¡Aplauso!

Hispanic Children's Theater

Edited by Joe Rosenberg

PIÑATA
BOOKS

Arte Público Press
Houston, Texas
1995

possible through grants from the r the Arts (a federal agency), the Lila st Fund and the Andrew W. Mellon Foundation.

Acknowledgements for aid in locating some of the scripts go to Pedro Monje-Rafuls and Gilberto Saldívar.

Piñata Books
A Division of Arte Público Press
University of Houston
Houston, Texas 77204-2090

Piñata Books are full of surprises!

Cover design and illustrations by
Daniel Lechón

¡Aplauso! : Hispanic children's theater / [edited] by Joe
Rosenberg.
       p.   cm.
    Summary: A collection of plays for children, writ-
ten in English and Spanish by Hispanic American
authors.
    ISBN 1-55885-136-4 : ISBN 1-55885-127-5 (pbk.) :
$7.95
    1. Children's plays, American—Hispanic American
authors. 2. Hispanic Americans—Juvenile drama. [1.
Hispanic Americans—Drama. 2. Plays—Hispanic
American authors.] I. Rosenberg, Joe.
PS628.H57A65   1995
812'.540809282—dc20   94-36005
                                                  CIP
                                                   AC

The paper used in this publication meets the require-
ments of the American National Standard for Perma-
nence of Paper for Printed Library Materials
Z39.48-1984. ∞

¡Aplauso!

Hispanic Children's Theater

Edited by Joe Rosenberg

Contents

— Contents —

Introduction

By Hispanic theater in the United States we mean many things. We refer to theater scripts written entirely in Spanish, theater scripts written entirely in English, and bilingual scripts which combine these languages to various extents. By Hispanic theater we also mean theater that addresses Puerto Rican, Cuban American, and Mexican American life, as well as Hispanic Intercultural life of various descriptions: exile life, life of nostalgia for the past, life that is trying to bring the past into the present, life that is trying to find a future. And sometimes we mean all of the above. So it becomes evident that reading this sort of anthology offers the possibility of considering the scripts for production as plays.

There are a great many possibilities of production and staging offered by each script. A script is not a play. It is a suggestion for the play the reader can imagine to happen—and the magic word is not script, but *happen*. Until the moment of the play the script is an unfulfilled set of suggestions. Reading all these scripts together, however, presents the reader with a dimension none of the playwrights ever intended: for together all these scripts present a rich social document which can come to life on various stages, presenting what the several playwrights intended. The intentions are all written. They are in the scripts. The reader can use the intentions to weave simple and various degrees of complex social fabrics. And the possibilities of understanding Hispanic life through Hispanic theater are not even all here in this anthology. This is a fragment.

Because scripts are about human actions, actions usually involving the pursuit of adjustment to social conditions at moments of crisis, the various actions implied by the scripts in this anthology present a cosmos of interests and aspirations all of which may be called Hispanic-American, as distinguished from scripts that, let us say, present Scandinavian life in America. Yet it is potentially gratifying for the non-Hispanic to observe also that characters can be cast with Scandinavian Americans, for example, because there are at times clusters of experiences that are in common and sharable. And it can be gratifying also to observe, become aware of and learn that cultural differences do create legitimately different ways of communicating. These possibilities lead to friendliness past the "hello, how are you and have a good day" insulations of people who really do not want to get to know one another. The recognition of what goes on in others and the ability to assess similarities and differences can lead to deserved self-congratulation and a host of other conditions good for our egos. But perhaps even more important, they help to remove the paranoias created by hesitant encounters with the strange and unknown that threaten to tamper with and perhaps destroy our security.

Enrichment and cleansing, then, are the rewards of exposure to this social document. And there is no end to the possibilities of achieving enrichment: through reading the dialogue, through imagining the unspoken that creates the dialogue both of words and of silences, through acting out the script, which releases the actor and the public from the confining binds of a literal approach to the dialogue, through the more limited but still useful book in hand acting out, and finally through the discussion that can be initiated by every one of these processes. And it should not by any means be overlooked that the process can be very enjoyable, especially if it permits the imaginations of young people to take hold, something that makes acting more exciting and attractive to people of all ages than, say, the descriptive literature to be encountered in some books dealing with social conditions.

The writers of most of these scripts, being the products of two cultures, are also among the enriched by virtue of their dual heritage because they are privileged to be able to dialogue with each culture and to interdialogue. They offer as a result a certain unique aspect of their American heritage. It is a way of offering to other Americans not like themselves such enlightenments as a tribal way of considering the growth of an oak tree, a way of interpolating the age-old legend of the Llorona that pervades the mythology of much of Latin American life, a way of understanding about such seeming stereotypes as the Uncles Pánfilo and the burros who are not all alike and are as different as people sometimes are, a way of presenting the cost of conformity to be paid by a dissident cat if he decides to enter the mainstream, a way of imparting somewhat non-mainstream wisdom to a child bent on economic aggrandizement, which is sometimes an inferior type of aggrandizement, a way of understanding about cosmic racketeers who carry free enterprise a little too far. Such observations are specific contributions to the panorama of social literature. It is as if the reader can feel that by ingesting what may be different about life he/she becomes more than he/she was; and by sharing the banquet of what is to be understood in common, he/she feels larger and more complete.

The only one of these scripts not by an American is "Microbios," by the distinguished Mexican playwright, Emilio Carballido. It is included for several reasons. One is that Carballido's script is universal in its message to children: it puts the idea of personal hygiene attractively to all. Another is that this script, like Manual Martín's "The Legend of the Golden Coffee Bean," offers teachers of science an attractive alternative for achieving targeted interest. Still another is that it is the only script entirely in Spanish, and in that way serves as an excellent teaching device, especially when acted. And of course, finally, it offers those who wish to present plays an exceptionally fine script that suggests the use of exciting stage magic.

In summation, this anthology offers many opportunities: scripts for plays, scripts for readings, scripts for language study, monolingual scripts in Spanish and in English, bilingual scripts, and scripts from various cultures subsumed under the heading of Hispanic. Some of these scripts can be acted for children by adult actors, others can be acted by children and/or shared with adult actors. All can be read for their rich contribution to the American image.

The introduction to each script provides specifics about the nature and potential of the script.

¡Aplauso!

Hispanic Children's Theater

Edited by Joe Rosenberg

Fred Menchacha and Filemón

by

José G. Gaytán

Fred Menchacha and Filemón
by José G.Gaytán

Hey, amigos!! I am muy contento, very happy to be here with you.

But I cannot stay very long. You see, I had to leave my marranos, my pigs, my chickens, and my gallinas alone at the rancho. If I do not hurry back to feed them, they may get out of the corral and eat the corn and the frijoles I planted in the field. ¡Son muy malos los animales! The animals are very mean. They can eat my casa and my petate.

I also had to leave my donkey, my Filemón, on the other side of the border. I wanted to bring him here to meet you, but the man at the border, he said he needed his chots.

"What is the chots for, señor," I asked.

"He may be sick!"

"Oh no! My donkey is no sick...He is as healthy as a horse!!"

"No le hace," the man said. So I had to leave him tied to a pole. I hope nobody steals him.

Oh, I forgot to introduce myself. This is muy bad manners. You can call me Fred Menchacha.

Did you know that to cross the border from Mexico you need a pasaporte, a passport? When I crossed the bridge, the officer at the border, he said: "Dame tus papeles, give me your papers." So I took out my newspaper and I gave it to him.

"No, not your newspaper. Your papers, your passport!"

"Oh, I do not have a pasaporte, señor..."

"Well then, you cannot come inside the United States."

"But I have to come inside, señor. The children at (*name of institution*) are waiting for me."

"Okay, then, I will give you a temporary permit, but you must come back as soon as you finish, and give me back the permit, otherwise you can go to jail."

My donkey, my Filemón and I, we have been many places. One time, we got on a big chip and went across the ocean to a country called France. Have you heard of it? Over there the people they like to hug you and kiss you on the cheek when they say "hello."

When we got off the big chip, the French people, they said, "Bon jour, Filemón, Bon jour, Fred Menchacha." And they came to me and gave me a great big hug and a kiss.

At first I was not too, how you say, comfortable, but before you know it, I was hugging and kissing people too. Hugging is good for you! It's good for your health! Unless you hug someone who does not like to be hugged. Yes, when I was in France I could hug anyone, but when I came back to Mexico, and I said hello to my uncle Panfilo with a hug and a kiss, and he pushed me back, and he said, "Si me vuelves a abrazar, ¡te doy un moquete!"

But over there in France, the people liked me so much that they wrote me a song. Have you heard it? It has my name on it! It goes like this:

Fred Menchacha, Fred Menchacha,
Dormez-vous, Dormez-vous?
Sonnez les matines, sonnez les matines,
Ding, dang, dong.
Ding, dang, dong.

You heard it? You want to sing it with me? Okay.

(Repeat song, accompanied by the children.)

Bueno, I had better go check on my Filemón. I left him alone too long. I hope he hasn't kicked anyone. He kicks very hard, muy duro! One time, he and I were going to a fiesta in the village. I was riding on his back. It was time for my siesta. I got a little sleepy, and I led my Filemón straight into a cactus. He got thorns on his nose, and he got very mad at me. He started jumping up and down, and I fell on my cabeza. Then, when I was getting up, he kicked me on my, "cómo se llama," right here *(Points to his bottom)*.

Ever since then, I do not take my siesta when I am riding on my Filemón.

18

The Caravan

by

Alvan Colón

The Caravan
by Alvan Colón

This play for children was initially based on the poem "La Elegía del Saltimbanqui," by the Puerto Rican poet Luis Palés Matos.

The version that follows was written by Alvan Colón Lespier in Spanish with songs and some dialogue in English.

During performances for school children, Los Pregones developed a version totally in English, one in Spanish and one bilingual.

The play can be performed with a minimum of three actors and two musicians.

The basic costume for all performers is the traditional Vejigante costume and masks of the Feasts of Santiago of the coastal regions of the island of Puerto Rico. When interpreting other characters, the actors don particular elements that define that character, i.e., top-hat, cape, hats, ribbons and a bright umbrella.

The music is based on typical coastal rhythms, plena *and* bomba, *and the instruments are:* pan-deros *(hand held drums), congas, accordion and drum set, (trap set is sufficient).*

The set consists of a bare stage and a six-foot folding ladder which is painted in bright colors.

Characters

VEJIGANTE
MR. SALTIMBANQUI
BEATRIZ
MARTIN THE FISHERMAN
MUSICIAN 1
MUSICIAN 2

Musicians are on-stage, and Vejigante *is sitting on the top step of the ladder.*

Saltimbanqui *and* Beatriz *enter singing.*

We've been travelling for many days
hoping to reach our destiny.
We'll know we're there when we can see
the shining lights and crowded streets.
Oh how we long for greater speed
that we may show our magic deeds.
We'll know we're there when we can see
the shining lights and crowded streets.

Music continues.

SALTIMBANQUI: Yo man, chill out...I'm in control here!
BEATRIZ: I think we should look for...
SALTIMBANQUI: I know the way, just follow me!

BEATRIZ: Please let me see the map *(Takes map, looks at it)*. Oh no, we're really lost. What are we going to do now?

SALTIMBANQUI: *(Taking back the map and pointing the way with the umbrella.)* Have no fear. I am the one and only, the great Mr. Saltimbanqui and I will lead the way. I see the lights! Charge!

VEJIGANTE: *(Leaping from the ladder.)*

Toco, toco, toco, toco,

Vejigante come coco,

Vamos muchachos pa' la marina

A comer pan y sardinas.

SALTIMBANQUI: Don't gimme none of that coco stuff. Besides I don't like sardines. But on the other hand, if you help me out, I'll give you a reward.

VEJIGANTE: So you were saying you needed help?

SALTIMBANQUI: My name is Mr. Saltimbanqui and this here is my helper, Beatriz. We started our journey many days ago. We walked through valleys and mountains without stopping, searching for the great city...when all of a sudden we were caught in a giant storm...

VEJIGANTE: Don't you have a map?

SALTIMBANQUI:Of course we do, but it's an old one and Beatriz forgot to change it!

BEATRIZ: *(Aside.)* Ha! He doesn't know the difference an old map and a new one. You see he doesn't know how to read.

VEJIGANTE: Very well...*(Makes a gesture with his hand as if asking for money.)* but...

SALTIMBANQUI: I'll pay you when we get to the city. There's a lot of money there.

BEATRIZ: But you have money, I saw it!

SALTIMBANQUI: Don't pay any attention to her, she's still a little dizzy from the storm.

VEJIGANTE: I don't need any money, but if you tell me a story...

SALTIMBANQUI: I don't know any stories. *(To Beatriz.)* Do you know any?

BEATRIZ: This little piggy went to market, this little piggy stayed home, etc. *(Or any other children's story.)*

VEJIGANTE: Very well. What you have to do now is follow that trail to the edge of the river. There you will meet Martin the Fisherman. Tell him that I sent you and ask him if he will take you to the other side of the river on his boat.

As Saltimbanqui *and* Beatriz *walk to the river bank,* Vejigante *puts on the Martin Fisherman hat and cape, lays the step ladder on its side, making a row boat out of it, and sits on it as if he were fishing.* Saltimbanqui *and* Beatriz *arrive and meet* Martin.

SALTIMBANQUI: Are you Martin the Fisherman? I am Mr. Saltimbanqui and this here is my helper Beatriz. Vejigante sent us. He said you will help us get to the other side of the river so we can get to the great city of Onglishtown.

MARTIN FISHERMAN: Well, if Vejigante sent you, it's okay. Hop in. But you must help me row. *(He hands* Saltimbanqui *a paddle.)* You do know how to row, don't you?

SALTIMBANQUI: Sure I do. *(He takes the paddle, looks at it and hands it to* Beatriz. *They row across the stage to the tune of "Row, row your boat." They arrive at the other side and quickly get out of the boat.)* This is it, my faithful friends. *(To* Beatriz *and* Martin.*)* We are here at last, and just as I promised, I will make you so rich and famous that all your wishes will come true!

BEATRIZ: Hear ye! Hear ye! Attention everybody. This is the great Mr. Saltimbanqui who travels from town to town with his famous magic tricks...and I am Beatriz his helper.

SALTIMBANQUI:
I'm Mr. Saltimbanqui,
the master of the Caravan.
This is Beatriz, my faithful helper.
I'll show you tricks
that'll make you tremble.
I'm Mr. Saltimbanqui,
the master of the Caravan.

And now I will need your utmost cooperation...
(To Martin.*)* Hey you!

MARTIN: Who me?

SALTIMBANQUI: Of course, who else? Here. *(Hands him a large page of a newspaper.)* Now, hold this with both hands. I will take ten steps and with my invisible whip will cut the paper in two. *(Drum roll as* Mr. Saltimbanqui *takes the steps backwards.* Beatriz *blindfolds him. He grabs an imaginary whip and takes a couple of practice swings and then slashes the newspaper in two.)* Very well, that will be twenty-five cents, please!

MARTIN: Do you mean that I have to pay you?

SALTIMBANQUI: Of course, what did you think, that I was doing all this for free?

MARTIN: Wait a minute! I did half and you did half. Besides, you wouldn't have been able to do it without me, because I was the one that brought you here. Therefore, you have to pay me!

SALTIMBANQUI: Are you crazy? I am the great Mr. Saltimbanqui, the one and only Saltimbanqui. This is only the beginning...Now, Beatriz, my helper, will walk the tight rope. *(Together they stretch a piece of rope, raise in the air, then lay it flat on the floor, and as the drum rolls,* Beatriz *walks on it from end to end.)*

BEATRIZ: Now, the one and only Mr. Saltimbanqui will perform a death defying trick. He will jump from atop the ladder and dive head first into this cup of water!!! *(Drum roll,* Saltimbanqui *climbs the ladder, concentrates and jumps feet-first towards the cup.* Beatriz *tries to entice the audience to applaud. Seeing the reaction,* Saltimbanqui *snaps his fingers and with a loud clap casts a spell over* Beatriz.*)* And now, pay close attention. The powers of Mr. Saltimbanqui are limitless. Mr. Saltimbanqui will now take you to the magical world of, of... *(As in a daze.)*

SALTIMBANQUI: Mental telepathy, stupid!

BEATRIZ: Mental telepathy, stupid.

SALTIMBANQUI: No, no, no, you, not them!

BEATRIZ: I'm hungry, I'm thirsty, I'm tired and I want to rest.

SALTIMBANQUI: *(Snaps his fingers again and regains control over* Beatriz.*)* I am a man of my word and always fulfill my promises and, for just a few cents more, I will show you something never seen before. My assistant Beatriz will blindfold me, she will go into the audience and I will read her mind!

BEATRIZ: *(She goes into the audience and follows the agreed-upon sequence of naming child, green and circle.)* Very well Mr. Saltimbanqui, what am I pointing at?

SALTIMBANQUI: A boy/girl.

BEATRIZ: What color is this shirt/sweater?

SALTIMBANQUI: Green/blue/red.

BEATRIZ: And now Mr. Saltimbanqui will perform the most difficult telepathic feat of all. Concentrate, Mr. Saltimbanqui, concentrate and tell me what is the shape that I am describing?

SALTIMBANQUI: A circle!

BEATRIZ: Mr. Saltimbanqui, I'm thirsty, I'm tired, I'm hungry...I can't take this anymore. *(*Saltimbanqui *was pushing* Beatriz *too far without knowing what would happen.)*

SALTIMBANQUI: And now my dear friends, Beatriz will entertain you with... *(*Beatriz *faints.)* What's happening, Beatriz? We're in the middle of a show. Come on, get up! Let's get to work. You can't do this to me! Okay, if that's the way you want it, it's fine with me... You are fired! *(To* Vejigante) Hey you, you want a job?

VEJIGANTE: I already have a job. I sing the stories of my people.

SALTIMBANQUI: And you call that work? Nobody pays attention to your stories. Besides, they are not important...BORING! Who cares about the past, about what happened a long time ago?

VEJIGANTE: *(To the audience.)* Is that so? Do you care about the past? Do you care about the stories of our people? *(Improvise with audience.)*

SALTIMBANQUI:

Stories for me? Ha!

I know who I am

I am how I am.

I don't need books.

I don't have to read.

You don't have to learn,

You don't have to think,

Because you've got me!

BEATRIZ: You don't understand. I don't want to waste my time. I want to learn about history and science...it's important.

SALTIMBANQUI: Yo man, important is what you eat, what you feel...that's important! Look, I know a lot of things and I have them up here. If you stay with me, you won't have to learn anything. I will do the thinking for you.

BEATRIZ: But if I don't think I won't learn and I won't grow.

SALTIMBANQUI: You've already grown!

BEATRIZ: But I want to grow inside.

SALTIMBANQUI: If you grow inside, you'll pop like a balloon!

BEATRIZ: Well, I'm leaving. So pay me what you owe me.

SALTIMBANQUI: Are you sure you want to leave? You'll be all alone.

BEATRIZ: I won't be alone. Besides, if I need help, there's Vejigante.

SALTIMBANQUI: Okay, but don't say I didn't warn you. *(He gives her a few coins.)*

BEATRIZ: *(Taking the coins in her hand, sings.)*
Is this it, is this it?
I think I deserve much better.
I worked hard, very hard.
I think I deserve much better.

SALTIMBANQUI: Chill out!

BEATRIZ: But you promised you would pay me for my work.

SALTIMBANQUI: And I did!

BEATRIZ: This is only forty-seven cents! Where's the rest?

SALTIMBANQUI: Well, I used it to buy my...our food, our costumes...

BEATRIZ: These costumes are all worn out!

SALTIMBANQUI: How dare you contradict me? Ungrateful. You were nobody till you met me. Everything you know you owe to me. I showed you the world, I fed you, I gave you a place to sleep... When you are with me, that's all the money you need...and just imagine how I feel. Put yourself in my position....

VEJIGANTE: *(Leaping from the ladder, casts a spell over* Saltimbanqui *and freezes him.)*

Toco, toco, toco, toco,
Vejigante come coco.

BEATRIZ: *(She walks over to* Saltimbanqui *and takes his top hat and cape.)* Now I'm going to myself in your position and see how it feels.

SALTIMBANQUI: Wait a minute! Hold it, I don't like this game, no, no, stop. Hey what the...

BEATRIZ:
Oh! Mr. Saltimbanqui
You lied about the Caravan
You fooled them all
You fooled us all
Now I don't fear you anymore!

You used your tricks to buy me out
to make me work for nearly nothing
But now you see how things have changed
And you will have to take my place!

VEJIGANTE: And as we say in Puerto Rico...we flipped things around! *(Now* Beatriz *is in command and* Saltimbanqui *is under her control.)*

SALTIMBANQUI: Ladies and gentlemen, it is with great pleasure that we present the great, the one and only Beatriz.

BEATRIZ: Thank you, thank you... And now my assistant Saltimbanqui will perform the death-defying mortal leap...

SALTIMBANQUI: I'm tired, I'm hungry, I'm thirsty, I want to rest...

BEATRIZ: Come on. Get up! You can't do this to me....

VEJIGANTE: Beatriz, what are you doing?

BEATRIZ: When I was tired, he made me do things and made me work...so now I am going to... *(Veji-gante freezes the action. He improvises with the audience and asks questions about the change. Is this the best way to change things, are there other ways, other solutions to the problem?)*

ACTRESS: Well, Beatriz sure changed things around. If you noticed, when she took Saltim-banqui's place and took his power, she started to do the same things to him that he used to do to her.

ACTOR: So in reality, things didn't change at all.

ACTOR : All they did was change places.

ACTRESS: And changing places is really not changing things if you are just going to do the same things that were done to you.

VEJIGANTE:

Toco, toco, toco, toco.

Vejigante come coco.

(Actors assume positions previous to the freeze, and when Vejigante *gives the word, they resume the play.)*

BEATRIZ: I think the caravan can belong to both of us.

SALTIMBANQUI: Both of us? Never, never. I am Mr. Saltimbanqui, the one and only...

BEATRIZ: But both of us do the work, so both of us should share the money and the fame.

SALTIMBANQUI: Never. I will never give up!

BEATRIZ: But you have nothing to give up because I took it all! I am in control...but I think we can work together, as equals.

SALTIMBANQUI: As equals? I need a helper...

BEATRIZ: I will help you and you will help me.

SALTIMBANQUI: Well, I don't know...

BEATRIZ: And if you get any ideas about going back to what you were doing before...forget it, it's over, forever! Deal?

SALTIMBANQUI: Deal!

ALL: *(Sing.)*

Toco, toco, toco, toco.
Vejigante come coco.

Vamos muchachos pa' la marina
A comer pan y sardinas.

Bocón

by

Lisa Loomer

Bocón*

by Lisa Loomer

Characters

ACTOR 1
ACTOR 2
ACTOR 3
ACTOR 4
ACTOR 5
MIGUEL
JUDGE
ROSITA
VENDOR 2
VENDOR 3
CECILIA
ANA
LA LLORONA
LUIS

*"Bocón" was commissioned by the Improvisational Theatre Project, Director Peter C. Brosius, the Theatre for Young People of the Mark Taper Forum.

VILLAGER 1
VILLAGER 2
VILLAGER 3
REFUGEE
SHROUD
NIGHT
DUENDE
VIEJITA 1
VIEJITA 2
VOICE KEEPER
VOICE PICKER

Prologue

*The play opens with a rhythmic spoken song—
an invitation, and a challenge, to the audience. All
the Actors are in simple white clothes, suggesting a
chorus of campesinos. They each have two straw
sticks which punctuate the rhythms of the song. The
sticks are beaten against the floor, in the air, against
the sticks of another actor, creating movement to the
song.*

CHORUS: Imagine a land...
ACTOR 1: Fíjate, imagine!
CHORUS: Jaguars, papagallos...
ACTOR 2: Yellow corn in the fields . . .
CHORUS: Imagine a land...fíjate, imagine!
ACTOR 3: ¡Oye marimba!
ACTOR 4: ¿Quieres sandías?
ACTOR 5: ¡Mira: Quetzal en las ceibas allí!

CHORUS:
> Imagine a place...
> War in the mountains...

ACTOR 1: There's a war in the mountains!

ACTOR 2: Fire in the sky...

CHORUS:
> Imagine this place,
> Not far from here!

ACTOR 3: *(Whispered.)* Fíjate, imagine...

(Faster now.)

ACTOR 1: Cross the borders!

ACTOR 4: Take my story...

CHORUS: Cross the borders...

ACTOR 5: Take my hand!

CHORUS: *(Fading now.)*
> Take my story, take my story...

(Whispered.)

Fíjate, imagine...

Scene One

Night. The stage is bare and dark. Miguel *enters and begins to run from an invisible border guard. The* Chorus *can create a border with their sticks, stopping him. Once the guard speaks, they exit.*

BORDER GUARD'S VOICE: *(Out of breath.)* Stop! That's it, kid. Now, you hold up right there.

Miguel *stops. We should feel that a bird is being captured: one of* Miguel's *arms is lifted up, then the*

*other, like wings. Then both arms are brought down
and back behind him, and the chase is over.*

The Judge *enters behind a scrim, larger than
life. Or he, too, may be just a voice. He bangs his
gavel. The sound echoes.*

JUDGE: What's your name, son? *(Miguel is too
frightened and confused at first to speak.)* Where
are you from? Guatemala? El Salvador? *(Pause.)*
Who brought you here? Your parents? Where
are your parents, son? *(Louder and slowly.)* ¿Sus
padres? ¿Dónde están sus padres? *(He clears his
throat.)* Look, I am a judge, son, and I have to
know where you come from. How am I supposed
to know where to send you back to, if I don't
know where you're from? *(More insistent.)* What
are you afraid of? Where are your parents?
(Faster.) Why don't you speak up, son? Who
brought you here? What are you afraid of?
WHERE ARE YOU FROM!? *(The last line
echoes. The* Judge *bangs his gavel, and we hear
the boot sound that* Miguel *hears in his
mind.*Miguel *starts to tell the* Judge *his story,
awkwardly. As he gets more comfortable, the
story is directed more and more to the audience.)*

Scene Two

MIGUEL: Yo vengo de...es un pueblito...I come
from a small village, San Juan de la Paz—in the
middle of my country—by the river they call La
Ballena, because the river swells up sometimes like
a fat green whale...and we...all the people there

work for Don Madera, picking his coffee for him in the fields and... *(Smiling.)* My father says he can't pick his own coffee 'cause his belly is so big, he... *(He sticks his belly way out so he can't see or reach over it.)* can't find the basket! *(He laughs at his own joke, but no one else does. So he explains.)* To put the coffee beans in, pos... *(Embarrassed.)* Bueno...After you're done working, you could go to the plaza, where there's always people selling...

From offstage, we hear the Vendors *singing their wares, softly, beckoning* Miguel's *memory.*

ROSITA: *(Off.)* ¡Pupusas!
VENDOR 2: *(Off.)* ¡Bananas!
VENDOR 3: *(Off.)* ¡Flores!

Rosita, Cecilia *and the two other* Vendors *begin to enter and spread out their wares. The foods they are selling might be stuck to blankets which can be unfurled, as memory is unfurled, in a swirl of color and movement.*

CECILIA: ¡Tamales!
ROSITA: ¡Aguacates!
VENDOR 3: ¡Piñas!
VENDOR 2: ¡Aguas frescas!
ROSITA: ¡Manzanas!

Miguel *takes a bunch of firecrackers from his pocket, a self-styled vendor, and joins in the scene in the plaza.*

MIGUEL: Firecrackers! ¡Cohetes! ¡Para la Fiesta de San Juan! The saints love firecrackers!

That's how they know there's a fiesta! Then they come down from the sky... *(Grabbing a pupusa.)* and they eat a pupusa... *(An invitation to the sky.)* Que vengan a la fiesta—¡todos los santos gordos!

VENDOR 2: ¡Miguel!

MIGUEL: *(Still talking about the saints.)* And they drink a Coca-Cola... *("Drunk" now, dancing.)* and they dance with all the ladies...

CECILIA: Ay, he's got a Big Mouth...

ROSITA: *(Eating a pupusa.)* ¡Bocón!

MIGUEL: ¡Sí! Saints, come down, before Rosita eats all the food in the village! Come sing...

CECILIA: Not so loud, Bocón, the Soldiers will hear you.

MIGUEL: *(But this only makes him more rambunctious, and he starts to sing a child's song, changing the words to mock the soldiers. Singing defiantly.)* Chanca barranca, hojitos de laurel, Soldiers of my village, soldados de papel!

CECILIA: *(Frightened.)* ¡Cállate! Quiet!

MIGUEL: *(To audience, still giddy.)* The Soldiers didn't like us to sing... *(*Kiki El Loco *enters, and prepares for his dance.)* Or dance... *(The tone of the scene changes:* Kiki *is as much a part of the spirit world as of this one.)* But there was an old Indian, Kiki El Loco, who used to dance all the time at fiestas—right in the plaza! They say he was deaf. But he could hear music right through the ground—like a radio! (*Kiki *begins to dance. It's part folk dance, part wizardry, part protest. The others watch in awe—and some fear.)*

CECILIA: *(Worried.)* Mira ese Kiki El Loco, how many times have the Soldiers told him, "Don't dance!"

MIGUEL: He's not afraid of nothing! Mira: the Dance of the Quetzal! The Bird of Freedom! *(Suddenly we hear the sound of the Boot...and helicopters. Miguel becomes terrified.)* ¡Los Soldados! The Soldiers! *(The others run off, frightened.)*

ANA: *(Offstage.)* ¡Miguel!

MIGUEL: *(Calling, without moving.)* ¡Sí, ahorita vengo Mamá! *(We hear the Boot again, closer. In a fierce whisper.)* ¡Kiki, allí vienen los Soldados, Kiki! The Soldiers! *(Kiki stomps into the background, defiantly. As he dances off, he gives Miguel a magnificent red and green feather. The boot sound fades. He says to audience.)* The feather of the Quetzal! *(Looking after Kiki, with wonder.)* Kiki—he danced the Soldiers away! He's not afraid of nothing! *(He starts to sing again, fearless.)*

CHANCA BARRANCA,
HOJITOS DE LAUREL,
SOLDADOS DE MI TIERRA,
SOLDADOS GO TO...

ANA: *(Offstage.)* Miguel! Come in now or La Llorona's gonna get you!

MIGUEL: *(Terrified now.)* La Llorona...

Scene Three

Ana *runs on and pulls* Miguel *to another part of the stage, and we are in their house. She lays their petates (mats) and blankets on the floor, then begins to wash* Miguel *in a basin, as he struggles to tell the audience about* La Llorona.

MIGUEL: *(To audience.)* Ay, La Llorona, everybody in the village talks about her—the witch! "The Weeping Woman!" They say...

ANA: She killed her own children! *(She is killing* Miguel's *poor ears, scrubbing.)*

MIGUEL: ¡Verdad, Mamá!

ANA: Hundreds and hundreds of years ago. They say she drowned them in a river! *(She nearly drowns* Miguel.)*

MIGUEL: ¡Ay, Mamá, por favor!

ANA: And then she was sorry. She was so sad, she's been going all over the world, weeping for centuries—crying: *(Bloodcurdling.)* "¡Ay, mis hiiii-jos!"

MIGUEL: *(Imitating* La Llorona.*)* "My children! My children!"

ANA: *(Ana gets him under the blankets. The basin is turned over and covered with a cloth, becoming an altar. Scary.)* And if you're outside after dark...she'll think you're one of her children...and she'll grab you, and take you down to the river, too! *(Her tone changes completely, and she's just a regular, loving mom. Sweetly.)* Good night, Miguel. *(Ana lies down beside him and sighs. And then we hear, in the wind.)*

41

LA LLORONA'S VOICE: ¡Ay, mis hiiiiiijos!

MIGUEL: *(Miguel jumps three feet in the air. Gesturing wildly, a one-man show.)* ¡Mamá! I saw her! La Llorona—right outside—allí! She was all dressed in black...and she was ten feet tall...and she was floating on the air, Mamá! she had a face like death, como La Calavera— *(He makes a face.)* así! And teeth like a dog... And she put a magnet in me... *(Hand to his heart.)* here! And she was pulling me... Right down. To the river. And she was crying, ¡Ay, mis hiiiijos!"

ANA: Cálmate, Miguel. *(She pulls him down. She sighs as if to say, "what a nut." She crosses herself. They try to sleep. And then we hear...)*

LA LLORONA'S VOICE: ¡Ay, mis hiiiijos! *(Both of them sit straight up, scared out of their minds, crossing themselves madly.)*

ANA: *(Not too sure.)* It was just the wind, m'hijo, nada más. Duérmete con los ángeles, ¿sí? *(She sings a lullaby to calm her son.)*

A la ru-ru, niño,
a la ru-ru ya...
duérmese mi niño...

(After a few more bars, Luis *enters.)*

LUIS: *(Gravely.)* Ana... *(*Ana *goes to him.)* Kiki El Loco has disappeared.

MIGUEL: *(Miguel pops up again. To audience.)* Kiki—he disappeared!? *(A cry.)* NO!

Scene Four

A rooster crows and it is dawn. Miguel gets up and comes downstage to the audience.

MIGUEL: A lot of people were disappearing in my village. *(Luis begins to sharpen his machete. Ana rolls up the blankets and starts to prepare tortillas, as Miguel continues.)* But how do people disappear, Papá? Does the earth just open up and suck them in? Or...or maybe it's the duendes that trick people into their caves...or one of those ships that come down from the sky...or maybe it's the...

LUIS: *(A gentle hand over his son's mouth.)* Soldiers.

MIGUEL: *(Softly.)* I know . . .

LUIS: Vámonos. *(Ana sprinkles holy water in the four corners of their house, and exits. Miguel has his machete and guitar. He starts to go in the wrong direction. Luis turns him around for the thousandth time.)*

LUIS: El Norte, Miguel. North. *(They walk.)*

MIGUEL: But why are the Soldiers so angry with us, Papá? If the Soldiers are supposed to protect us, why is everybody afraid of them?

LUIS: It's a long story.

MIGUEL: *(To the audience.)* A lot of my father's stories were long, but it was a long walk to the fields...

LUIS: When the earth was about your age, there was only one man... Adam.

MIGUEL: *(Cutting in.)* I know—the guy who ate the apple—and then he said, "This apple is so good I'm going to…"

LUIS: *(Clapping a hand over* Miguel's *mouth again.)* "…sell it." *(His story is punctuated by their machetes.)* Well, God didn't like Adam selling his apples, because they weren't Adam's apples.

MIGUEL: *(Chuckling.)* "Adam's apples…"

LUIS: *(Gives him a look.)* They were the earth's apples. And God was so angry he took his machete and chopped Adam in three…

MIGUEL: ¡Como una manzana!

LUIS: And God said, "Adam, I'm going to take your head, Adam, and out of your head I'm going to make the Rich Man. Just a Big Head…and a pair of hands for grabbing. Then I'm going to take your arms and your back, Adam, and make the Poor Man. And the Poor Man will work the fields to put food in the Rich Man's mouth. A ver, ¿qué falta, what's left?…"

MIGUEL: The foot! ¡Sí! And…God said, "Adam, I'm going to take your foot, Adam, and out of your foot I'll make…"

LUIS: "The Soldier." *(Laughing.)* "And the Soldier will kick the Poor Man to do the Rich Man's work forever!" Y ya, m'hijo, that's the world. *(Beat.)* Pos, Adam forgot that he used to be one man, and all that's changed in thousands of years…is now the Soldier's got a boot. *(Laughing.)* And a dirty one too! ¡Y fea! ¡Y cochina, también!

MIGUEL: Papá, not so loud, Papá, the Soldiers will hear you, they'll think you're laughing at them!

LUIS: *(Laughing.)* But I am! I am laughing at them! Big ugly boot...fea...¡y apestosa también! *(Beat.)* But one day, the Poor Man's going to put down his machete, m'hijo... *(He does.)* and use his arms to tell the Boot... *(Raising his arms.)* "NO MORE!" ¿Sí?

MIGUEL: Sí, Papá.

LUIS: *(Dead serious, as if to the Soldiers.)* "¡No más!" *(Beat.)* Eso. Soon. A trabajar...

MIGUEL: *(Tentatively, he takes the feather of the Quetzal from his pocket.)* Mira, Papá...

LUIS: The feather of the Quetzal...the Bird of Freedom! Vete, run, Miguel, and show your mother, tell her it's good luck!

MIGUEL: *(Starts to run.)* ¡Sí, Papá!

LUIS: *(Exits, singing.)* Brazos para trabajar... corazón para amar...semilla para plantar...esta voz para gritar...

Ana, Cecilia *and* Rosita *are washing sheets in the river.* Ana *turns to* Miguel.

MIGUEL: ¡Mira, mamá!

But they are busy washing and talking about...

CECILIA: *(Waving an envelope.)* Mira, Miguel, we got a letter from my daughter...

ANA: *(Overlapping.)* ¡En Los Angeles!

ROSITA: The City of Angels!

MIGUEL: Sí, pos... *(He tries to show them the feather.)* mira...

ROSITA: She said all the kids there got big mouths—just like you! Everybody in Los Angeles make a lot of noise!

CECILIA: They got radios in the cars, and they drive around all day in their villages playing music...

ROSITA: LOUD, so the angels could hear it in the sky!

MIGUEL: *(Still trying to show them the feather.)* Mira, Papá said...

CECILIA: Ay, you could hear your papá laughing all the way to the river. He better be careful...

ANA: He's a brave man, Cecilia.

CECILIA: Brave like Kiki El Loco. Y bocón, Ana... *(Indicating Miguel.)* como you know who...

MIGUEL: *(Proudly.)* ¡Sí! Mamá, MIRA... *(To audience, sadly.)* But I never got to show her, porque...

ANA: *(Ana hears something in the distance, and turns upstage, frightened. To audience.)* My mother wasn't listening, porque... *(Beat, an effort to avoid the memory.)* My mother, she can hear a baby cry in the next village... *(We hear the Boot, and Luis is propelled onto the stage. His hands are tied behind his back. Yelling, running to Luis.):* NO! ¡Déjelo por amor de Dios! No, YOU CAN'T TAKE HIM! NO! *(We hear the Boot. One of Ana's arms is lifted, then the other. Then both arms are pulled down behind her by an invisible soldier. We should feel that the Quetzal is being taken, the bird of freedom. The capture is like Miguel's in Scene 1.)*

MIGUEL: *(To audience, with great difficulty.)* And the Soldiers took my mother for talking loud, too. And I wanted to yell... *(He tries to yell, but his voice flies away in terror. We hear his "NO!" on tape, flying away, echoing and fading. He mouths wildly, silently.)* NO! NO!

ROSITA: *(To* Cecilia.*)* His voice, Mamá — IT FLEW AWAY! *(She runs off, scared. Ana and Luis are taken off, the sound of the Boot dragging them.)*

ANA: Run! M'hijo, run! I love you...

MIGUEL: *(Mouthing the word, silently.)* NO!

CECILIA: *(Cecilia grabs Miguel. She thinks and moves with lightning speed. This is not the first time She's had to send someone away from the soldiers, fast. In a rush, whispered.)* You have to run, Miguel—the Soldiers will be back! They'll make you join up with them, or they'll make you disappear.

MIGUEL: *(Miguel still cannot speak. He shakes his head wildly—"no!")*

CECILIA: *(Cecilia takes the envelope from California and stuffs it into is pocket.)* Here, take this. A hundred dollars my daughter sent me from Los Angeles—the City of Angels, Miguel! ¡Al norte! ¡Sí! They don't got soldiers there, Miguel—they got angels! That's where my daughter went, y tu también, that's where you'll go! *(He starts to run away from her. She grabs him.)* The Soldiers don't want us here, Miguel— we're not wanted in our own home! You tell the people there in Los Angeles...tell them we just want to work our land in peace! ¿Me entiendes?

Speak to me, Miguel, speak! *(Finally realizing.)*
¡Ay, no, por Dios! Your voice, Miguel, no! The
Soldiers...the Soldiers scared it away!? *(She hugs
him as tight as she can.)* It's hiding, m'hijo...it's
frightened... *(Dead serious.)* You've got to find it.
Don't let the Soldiers get your voice, Miguel!
Don't let it disappear! *(She hugs him once more,
and runs off.* Miguel *starts to run through the
village.The chorus appears, as* Villagers, *offering
directions as* Miguel *runs by.)*
VILLAGER 1: There is a forest . . .
VILLAGER 2: A Border of Lights . . .
VILLAGER 3: Then the City of Angels!
VILLAGER 1: Tell the people there . . .
VILLAGER 2: We got no more angels . . .
VILLAGER 1: Tell our story.
ALL:
 Tell our story...
 Tell our story...

Scene Five

The Journey

Miguel *runs and runs. When he stops, he is in a
strange, new world. [Note: All of the characters he
meets will be masked.] He looks around. Suddenly,
he hears...*

LA LLORONA'S VOICE: ¡Ay, mis hiiiijos!
VOICES: *(Offstage, frightened.)* ¡La Llorona...La
 Llorona! (Miguel *has no idea which direction to
 go in. He starts to go stage left. A Refugee enters
 from stage left, carrying her house on her back.)*

48

REFUGEE: Mira, don't go that way—los Solda-dos—the Soldiers! *(Miguel turns to go stage right. A* Shroud *enters from stage right.)*
SHROUD: Not that way! *(Pointing stage right.)* ¡LA LLORONA!

We hear the sound of a cat or a wild animal. Miguel *turns upstage. Behind the scrim, the figure of a woman rises up and spins, her rebozo [shawl] whirling in the wind, her endless hair flying in all directions:* La Llorona. *If stars can fly out of her hair, or lights can shoot from her fingertips, all the better.*

LA LLORONA: *(A frightening and haunting wail.)* ¡AY, MIS HIIIIJOS!

The wind howls. A figure in black enters in front of the scrim, hiding La Llorona. *This is* Night. *Now he turns to* Miguel—*who is out of his mind with fear—and starts to follow him, ominously, all over the stage. After a few moments, a face pops out of the wings, or from behind the scrim.* Miguel *never sees it, but it keeps reappearing in different places, under different hats. This is the green face of a being no more than three feet tall—the* Duende. *And his voice is as strange as his body.*

DUENDE: Psssst! ¡Oye! You tell him, "Get back, Night, don't hide La Llorona! Don't hide her!" *(But* Miguel *still cannot speak.* Night *advances.)* You got to trick the Night. Just pull down a star! Light a match, a candle... *(Miguel tries to follow the* Duende's *suggestions. He looks up at the sky... searches his pockets.)* Smile, pos, flash those white teeth! *(*Miguel *tries to smile. Night is not impressed. Thinking.)* A ver... Pretend it's the morning! What happens in the morning... uh... *(A hint.)* "Errr..." *(Beat.)* "Err..."

MIGUEL: *(Miguel can get his body to be a rooster, but his voice just won't help. Under his breath.)* Ay Dios... *(A perfect rooster imitation.)* Errr Errr Errr!

Night *runs for his life. The* Duende *dons a baseball cap, and strides over to* Miguel. *In a kinder world he'd be just a trickster, but in this one he's a shyster, preying on the bad luck of others, especially refugees.*

DUENDE: Pssst! ¡Oye, muchacho! No speaka the language, eh? *(Under his breath.)* Mocoso... *(Arm around* Miguel.*)* Need a coyote? Someone to take you north, amigo...show you the way! What... don't tell me, you thought I was a duende, right?

MIGUEL: *(Nods "yes.")*

DUENDE: *("Offended.")* Why, 'cause I'm short? All depends on your perspective! *(He extends to the actor's full height for a second.)* See what I mean? Short is very big now. *(He bobs up and down for emphasis.)* And short people make the finest coyotes in the world. Know why? 'Cause they're short! *(Under his breath.)* Mocoso... *(Patting Miguel on the head.)* Slip right under the border, whadda ya say? *(Miguel hesitates.)* Good! You mind going in my private DC10-7-11 jet? Right over... *(He spins* Miguel.*)* there! 'Course it's nothing fancy, just, oh, swimming pool, bullfight ring...pupusas... *(Yes,* Miguel *is interested...)* Got a couple of pesos for expenses? *(He shakes Miguel down, finding the envelope.)* ¡Fantástico! Let's see... *(Counting bills.)* There's food for the jet, fuel for the bulls...hotels, tips, chicklets... *(Miguel tries to fight for his money.)* Okay, I'll give you a break. I like you. *(He pretends to give him back a few bills.)* Tell you what. I'll warm up the jet, and I'll meet you right over... *(He spins* Miguel *again.)* there! *(*Miguel *is still reeling. He steadies himself. Checks his money. It's gone. He tries to shout after the* Duende. *But he has no voice to express his rage. He begins to search for his voice. He tries calling it, begging, commanding. Finally, he tries to summon it with his guitar. An* Old Woman *enters...we do not see her face.* Miguel *goes to her. She turns, rises to her full height—ten feet tall! It's..)*

LA LLORONA: *(A bloodcurdling wail.)* ¡Ay, mis hiiijos! ¡Córrele! *(*Miguel *is too scared to move.)* ¡Ay, mis hiiijos! Run hooooome! *(*Miguel *looks back towards home. He can't go there...)* ¡Ay, mis hiiijos! ¡CÓRRELEEEE! *(*Miguel *gathers all the strength he has, and shakes his head "no." He's saying no to the demon! He's not running home.* La Llorona *tears off her mask, incredulous. None has refused to run from her—in all her hundreds of years. She's completely thrown. In fact, She starts to sound like a regular woman. And without the mask she's about five-and-a-half feet tall. Exasperated, she says,)* Oye, tonto, ¿qué te pasa a ti, payaso? What does it take to send you home? Crazy kid... Híjole, ay, ay, ay, ay, ay... *(Miguel can't believe his eyes and ears.)* Why won't you go home, pues? *(Miguel explains, without words.)* You can't go home? *(Responding to his gestures.)* You'll die if you go home? *(Responding to more gestures.)* The Soldiers took your parents!? *(This is too much for her. And She bursts into tears. They don't call her "The Weeping Woman" for nothing. [Note: There is an elaborate ritual to her crying, a build and an explosion, so that each time we hear the build, it is increasingly comical.] Sputtering through tears.)* I...I try to scare you kids home so you'll be safe from the Soldiers. Now you're too scared to go home..."cause there are Soldiers there too! *(Miguel gestures, "Please stop crying.")* ¿Qué? You think it's easy going all over the world crying... *(Wailing.)* Ay mis hiiiijos"? *(Beat.)* Ay, it hurts. *(Hoarse.)* My throat's been killing me for a century. I'm up all night scaring children into their houses. I haven't had a good night's sleep in four hundred years! Not since the Conquistadores! But what else am I gonna do? ¿Qué más puedo hacer, eh? Speak! *(Beat.)* Oye, say something already or... *(This usually gets 'em.)* I'll drown you in the river... *(Miguel mimes frantically, "I've lost my voice!")* You've lost your voice? *(He continues, with gestures.)* The soldiers... scared it away? *(She starts to break down and cry all over again, but catches herself mid-wail.)* No. There's no time. *(Thinking out loud.)* You can't go home... pues, you've got to find your voice... *(To herself, tentative.)* Maybe I could help him... *(Insecure.)* Ay, no...pues, sí...pues, no...pues, sí...pues, no, pues...maybe just a little...just till he finds his voice? Okay. *(She goes to* Miguel.*)* Óyeme bien. The voices are trapped. Locked up in the Palace of the General! No one can get in! There's a gate of iron—high as the sky! And wild dogs, with teeth as sharp as razors! But the most dangerous...the most treacherous of all... is the Voice Keeper. He will trick you, and trick you...till you forget why you came, till you forget your own voice! Pues, you must not listen to him! *(*Miguel *mimes, "Not me.")* Not you. Good. Now, show me you can't be tricked...and I'll lead you to the Border of Lights! *(*Miguel *reacts: the Border of Lights! That's exactly where he wants to go!)* Apúrete, pues. To the Palace of the General! Y cuídate, be careful! *(Miguel starts to go in the wrong direction. She turns him around.)* Ay, por Dios, norte, north—¡allí! *(*Miguel *starts to walk, calling his voice with his guitar. Two* Viejitas *enter, arguing over where the voices are kept.)*

VIEJITA 1: Over that fence, mujer, under the volcano...

VIEJITA 2: No, no, behind the gate, in the General's Garden...that's where I've heard the voices...

VIEJITA 1: *(Noticing* Miguel.*)* Ay, why is he playing that guitar for? Dangerous! Peligroso...

VIEJITA 2: He's calling his voice, mujer!

VIEJITA 1: ¿Con la guitarra?

VIEJITA 2: Sí, he's calling his voice.

VIEJITA 1: ¡Muy peligroso!

VIEJITA 2: ¡Y loco también! *(To* Miguel.*)* You'll never get behind that gate, but if you do, watch out for the dogs!

VIEJITA 1: ¡Los perros, sí! *(The* Women *go off, howling like dogs.* Miguel *tries to get into the palace. He pounds on the iron gate. If an actual gate is not used, we hear the sound of his banging on an imaginary gate. He can hurt his hand, pounding on it. The* Voice Keeper *appears. If the* Duende *was a shyster, the* Voice Keeper *is a cool, smiling fascist. A Spaniard, with a sash full of medals, two huge* Guard Dogs *[actors in giant masks], and a black metal box full of voices.)*

VOICE KEEPER: Why all the noise, hermano!? The General is sleeping! Ssssshhhh! *(*Miguel *bangs on the gate.)* No, no, hermano! You don't want your voice—they're nothing but trouble! *(*Miguel *continues to try to get through the gate.)* That's why we keep them locked up...in here. *(Patting the box.)* The LOUD ones. The ones that TALK too much. *(Graciously.)* I'm the Voice Keeper. I keep things nice and quiet. For the General. *(He salutes in the direction of the palace.* Miguel *bursts through the palace gate. The* Dogs *growl. But the* Voice Keeper *tries to seduce* Miguel *with his words.)* The voices lie, hermano... they tell stories about the General...they get together, one voice starts in...and before you know it, every one of them has an opinion...there's a RACKET in the garden!...the General can't sleep. (Miguel *tries to get to the box. The* Voice Keeper *deftly keeps it away from him, sidestepping, doing a flamenco.)* Always complaining, crying, "I'm hungry!," whining, "It's not fair!" *(To the box of voices.)* Well, that's not our fault—we didn't make the world! (Miguel *manages to get the box open for a moment, and a murmur of voices flies out. The* Voice Keeper *quickly closes the lid. In a rage.)* ¡Infeliz! *(Recovering quickly, with a smile.)* Oyeme, hermano, the voices are happy now, content! They don't want to leave the palace! Listen for yourself... (Miguel *listens. He hears silence.)* Are they complaining? Nice and quiet now, peaceful now...no more shouting, mo more tears. A kinder, gentler garden... *(He removes a magnificent shiny medal from his sash and, very gradually starts to hypnotize* Miguel, *as he continues. hypnotizing, smooth.)* You don't want your voice, hermano... You don't want to wake the General... *(Sweetly.)* You don't want to tell bad stories about his Soldiers...Promise?... *(He is inadvertently hypnotizing the* Dogs *too.)* We're trying to protect you. The General loves you, hermanito! ¿Sí? You're a good boy...a quiet boy... Good. *(He teaches* Miguel *a gesture...a "sssshhh" and a thumbs-up.* Miguel *repeats the gesture, like a dazed, smiling Moonie. The* Voice Keeper *waves and gestures, exiting. The good* Moonie *waves and smiles back, repeating the gesture.* La Llorona *enters.* Miguel *repeats the gesture, smiling dumbly.)*

LA LLORONA: *(As if saying, "Oh, my God!")* ¡Ay, mis hijos! ¡Ay, m'hijo, qué te pasa a ti? Híjole. Ay, ay, ay, ay... You give up your fight? *(*Miguel *smiles and does the gesture the* Voice Keeper *taught him.)* For a pretty speech and a smile? *(*Miguel *smiles and gestures.)* And what will it be like when the whole world's quiet? Will you miss the voice of the guitar—the wind—the rain? Will you never hear the sound of your own voice telling the Soldier, "No!... No más"? *(*Miguel *smiles and gestures, thumbs up, again.)* NO!? *(She starts to cry. It builds, and builds, but She catches herself mid-wail.)* No. There's no time. *(The crying has broken the spell.* Miguel *is* Miguel. *The* Dogs *have awakened as well.)* I told you not to listen to him! *(She listens in the wind.)* Ay, listen... the voices! They flew away! *(We hear a murmur of voices, faint.)* No, they're frightened...they're hiding...at the edge of the earth... No! The Edge of the Sea! *(She listens. We hear the Boot, faint.)* ¡Oye! The Soldiers! You've got to find your voice, before the Soldiers do! *(The* Dogs *growl.)* Don't let them scare you! ¡Oye! Show me you can be brave—and I'll lead you to the BORDER OF LIGHTS! ¡Apúrete! To the Edge of the Seeeeaaa! *(He starts to go in the wrong direction. The* Voice Keeper *turns him around.)* ¡Al norte! North! ¡Allí! *(She calls up the ocean..and she's gone. We hear the sound of waves. Miguel plays his guitar, calling his voice. Instead, he catches a song.)*

VOICE PICKER'S VOICE: *(Offstage, singing.)* Nonantzin ih caucnimiquiz notle cuilpan xinech-toca...*(The* Voice Picker *wanders on, dragging a large net filled with seaweed, driftwood and shells. She looks like she's just come out of the sea herself. She's old and raggedy, and strange— like an old bag lady or ragpicker—but her rags are shells...and her shells are filled with lost voices. She speaks partly to herself, partly to* Miguel, *partly to the shells.)* Sigue, play, I like the old songs... *(Laughing.)* Don't tell the Soldiers... *(She starts to search the stage.)* You heard any voices by here? *(Confidentially.)* In the shells...that's where they like to hide. I got a sackful already, but the Soldiers won't be happy till I got 'em all... Greedy. And what do they pay me? Beans. *(Laughing.)* Frijoles, sí. Maybe a tortilla... *(She drags her net, searching.* Miguel *follows, curious, to the heavy net.)* Ay, break the back of an old woman. *(To* Miguel.*)* Pos, what else am I gonna do—find another husband to bring home the frijoles? I had three husbands! Now I got shells... *(Taking a shell from her pocket.)* This one I'm keeping, eh? Listen...

MAN'S VOICE IN SHELL: *(From the shell, we hear the* Voice of a Man, *amorous. The shell lights up when it speaks.)* Ay, mi amor, chula, preciosa, I adore you my love, I want to...

VOICE PICKER: *(She puts the shell back, quickly.)* Don't listen to that. You're too young. *(*Miguel *dives into the net of voices, looking for his.)* Oye, stop that, what are you doing? Muchacho feo, mocoso—those are my voices! I found them—for the Soldiers! Ay, break the heart of an old woman... (Miguel *mimes, "I'm looking for my voice!")* You're looking for your voice? Why didn't you say so? *(She looks him over.)* I'll help you. You seem like a good kid... *(Under her breath.)* y chulo, y precioso... *(She holds out the net, whispers.)* Bueno. Don't tell the Soldiers, eh? *(But in case there are any soldiers around, or anyone who'd tell the soldiers...she pretends she's a poor old woman being robbed blind.)* Ay, ay, steal from an old woman, aaaah! *(Sotto voce, to Miguel.)* Just one, eh? (Miguel *picks up a shell, and out flies...his own voice!)*

MIGUEL'S VOICE IN SHELL: *(Singing.)*
Chanca barranca, hojitos de laurel...
Soldados de mi tierra
Soldiers go to...

VOICE PICKER: *(Laughing.)* La voz de un loco, ¿sí? A crazy one! (Miguel *holds the shell high in the air, thrilled. He tips it and tries to pour the voice down his throat.)* Ay, that's your voice? *(To herself.)* He's got a big mouth... *(Suddenly, we hear the sound of the Boot. Terrified.)* The Soldiers! *(Running off.)* Don't tell the Soldiers where you got it, don't tell them! Por el amor de Dios!... *(We hear the Boot again.* Miguel *is so frightened, he throws the shell in the air. He dives for it as it falls...but misses. The shell shatters on the ground.* Miguel *tries to catch his voice, but it's flying away, fading. The Boot retreats. Silence. His voice is lost again. And*

Miguel *is completely alone.* Night *turns the stage dark.* Miguel *cries...but hears no sound. He touches his cheeks. No tears! He takes the feather of the Quetzal from his pocket and throws it on the ground in despair. He plays a line of Ana's lullaby on the guitar, to comfort himself.* La Llorona *enter, upstage, unseen by* Miguel. *She finds the feather and tucks it in her rebozo.* Miguel *stops playing. It is too painful to remember his mother.)*

LA LLORONA: *(Gently.)* Don't stop. That's a pretty tune. I remember... *(Vulnerable.)* I used to sing it to my own children. After a story... (Miguel *looks at her, amazed. Hesitant, shy.)* You...you think I can't tell a story? (Miguel *shakes his head "no.")* Pues, it's been a little while...three or four hundred years... *(She wants to comfort him, but she's been scaring people for centuries...and she's scared herself, now, to get close. Awkward.)* Would you...like to hear a story? (Miguel *shakes his head "no way." Continuing anyway.)* Bueno. Eh...once upon a time... *(She hesitates.)* That's how they start, sí? (Miguel *shrugs. Walks away. Warming up to it.)* Bueno. Once upon a time, there was a boy who lost his voice. And he went away, far away, and way down inside to find it. He even went to the Gate of the General! And he was very stu... *(Catching herself.)* very brave. But still he couldn't find his voice. So, he went all the way to the Edge of the Sea, and he found his voice in a shell! But the Soldiers came, and the boy was very scared... (Miguel *is insulted, shakes his head "no." La Llorona catches herself immediately.)* Very brave...but his voice was scared and flew away. Pues, the boy thought he'd lost his voice forever...and he was very sad, and he cried. *(Miguel is insulted and shakes his head "no!" Correcting herself.)* He almost cried. And it was a good thing he didn't, because his voice wasn't really lost! It was trapped somewhere, caught like a bird, just waiting for the boy to set it free. *(She starts to get up, but Miguel grabs her leg, as if to say, "Wait!—what then?")* What do you think happened? The boy kept looking for his voice, everywhere. Porque...who can live without a voice in this world, hombre? Without a voice, you have no story... No one knows where you come from, why you're here... Without your voice, you disappear! Is that what you want? *(Miguel shakes his head "no.")* Pues...it's your story...you find your voice and you tell me how it ends. *(Miguel asks, "But where do I look?")* You must look where you're most scared to go. You must look even in your darkest dreams... Oye, show me you have the courage to dream, and I'll lead you to the Border of Lights! Apúrate...to your dreams... *(He lies down and tries to dream. But he can't sleep.)* Ay, ay, ay, ay, ay. Now he wants a lullaby... *(She sighs. She clears her throat. She's shy.)* Pues, I haven't sung in a couple of hundred years...*(She starts to sing "La Llorona," the song men have sung about her for years and years, if not centuries. Singing softly.)*

Dicen que no tengo duelo, Llorona,
porque no me ven llorar...
dicen que no tengo duelo, Llorona,
porque no me ven llorar,
hay muertos que no hacen ruido, Llorona,
y es más grande su pena...

(Tiptoeing away.) Go m'hijo...to your dreams... (Miguel *sleeps.* Ana *enters, upstage, in* Miguel's *dream.)*

ANA: *(Singing.)* A la ru-ru, niño, a la ru-ru ya... (Luis *enters, puts down his machete and joins* Ana. *Neither is masked.)*

LUIS and ANA: *(Singing.)* Duérmese mi niño... *(A Military Calavera, a skeleton, comes up out of the earth, dancing to the lullaby. He puts a hand over* Miguel's Parents' *mouths, to silence them.* Miguel *runs to stop him.* La Calavera *turns on* Miguel *with his machete.)*

ANA: ¡No, déjelo, por el amor de Dios! *(*Miguel *grabs a branch, and he and* La Calavera *fight.* La Calavera *is winning. Just as he is about to finish* Miguel *off, just as his parents are about to disappear again!...* Miguel *speaks!)*

MIGUEL: *(To* La Calavera.*)* NO! NO, YOU CAN'T TAKE US! NO, YOU CAN'T STOP US! NO MÁS! *(The fight resumes...and this time* Miguel *wins!* La Calavera *goes back under the earth.* Miguel's Parents *raise their arms in slow motion, in exaltation...* La Llorona *runs on and shakes* Miguel. *His* Parents *slowly recede...)*

LA LLORONA: Wake up now, ¡despiértate, Miguel!

MIGUEL: *(He comes out of his dream, healed, talking a mile a minute.)* I did it! Yo gané. ¡Tengo mi voz! My voice! *(He spins* La Llorona *round and round.)* Chanca barranca, hojitos de laurel! Vámonos, apúrete, to the City of Angels! Got to tell the people there—we can stop the Soldiers! Got to tell our story—LOUD—so the angels can hear it in the sky!

LA LLORONA: Ay, he's got a big mouth. Bocón, ¿verdad?

MIGUEL: ¡Bocón! ¡Sí! Ay, what did they tell me? Which way? There's a forest... *(This is it.)* ¡Sí! And a border... Ay, cómo se llama ese border?— the Border of... *(He's shown her he has the courage to dream. She shows him the Border of Lights. With a wave of her arm, the downstage area fills with light.)* The Border of Lights! Ay, look at all those lights! ¡Vámonos! Let's go! *(There is a pause.)*

LA LLORONA: *(Sadly.)* I can't go with you, Miguel. I can't cross this border.

MIGUEL: ¿Cómo que no? You can do anything!

LA LLORONA: They don't believe in me up there. The children never hear my story...

MIGUEL: But...

LA LLORONA: *(Simply.)* How can you exist where people don't believe in you? The only way I can cross is in your heart.

MIGUEL: But, you've got to help me!

LA LLORONA: I have work to do at home in the villages, children to scare all over the continent.

MIGUEL: No lo creo, I don't think you want to scare children at all...

LA LLORONA: I don't want to scare them, I have to scare them. So they'll run in their houses and be safe from the Soldiers. I have to cry, "¡Ay, mis!" *(He puts his hand over his ears. She stops.)* Pues, who else is gonna do it? Everybody else is too busy just trying to survive.

MIGUEL: *(He takes a few steps away from her.)* Pos, I'm not going to cry...

LA LLORONA: Mira, do the clouds say, "I'm not going to rain?" *(For the first time in his journey,* Miguel *cries.)*

MIGUEL: I don't want to go alone.

LA LLORONA: Entiendo. I've been going alone for centuries. Who wants to go alone? Listen... *(He listens hard. In the wind, he hears...)*

ANA'S VOICE: Miguel! Come in now or La Llorona's gonna get you! *(*Miguel *and* La Llorona *smile.)*

LA LLORONA: Remember... *(*Miguel *listens again. He hears...)*

LUIS'S VOICE: But one day, m'hijo, the Poor Man will raise his arms, and tell the Boot, "¡No más!" "No more!"

MIGUEL: Papá!

LA LLORONA: Take them with you. Remember. *(A difficult revelation.)* Like I remember my children... Porque, when we remember the ones we love, we keep them alive, and free... *(*Miguel *nods.)* Go now. Tell your story.

MIGUEL: Gracias.

LA LLORONA: No, m'hijo, gracias a ti.

MIGUEL: No, pos, a usted, gracias.

LA LLORONA: No, no, gracias a ti.

MIGUEL: No, digo, a usted gra...

LA LLORONA: *(She starts to cry, catches herself.)* No. There's no time. *(She takes the feather of the Quetzal from her rebozo, and hands it to Miguel.)* Córrele, m'hijo, fly! *(Slowly, she heads back home , her feet never touching the ground. Miguel turns to the Border of Lights, and gets it right this time.)*

MIGUEL: *(Triumphantly.)* NORTH! *(He raises his arms in exaltation and in slow motion, he starts to cross the border. We hear the sound of helicopters. And Miguel's body goes from exaltation to fear. He starts to run. Again. The Chorus run on with their sticks, creating the border, stopping Miguel as they did in Scene 1.)*

Scene Six

There is a light change to indicate that we are back in the courtroom, where we began. If the figure of the Judge was seen behind the scrim in Scene 1, He will now appear. If not, we will just hear his voice. We hear the sound of the gavel.

MIGUEL: *(Still out of breath.)* And then, señor—Judge, digo—then a man in a uniform caught me...and he took me here. *(There is a long pause, the Judge clears his throat.)*

JUDGE: Well...that's quite a story. I've got to hand it to you, son, you kids have some pretty wild imaginations...

MIGUEL: Señor—*(Correcting himself.)* Judge, digo—are you going to send me back?

JUDGE: *(Chuckling.)* The things you kids come up with...

MIGUEL: *(Simply and without fear.)* If you send me home, I'll just come back again. I'm not going to disappear.

JUDGE: Of course not. *(Earnestly.)* People don't disappear up here, son. People only disappear in stories... (Miguel *touches the feather of the Quetzal, the rebozo* La Llorona *gave him...both quite real.)* We're just going to send you over to the Detention Center. Till we decide what we're going to do. *(The* Judge *bangs his gavel. We hear the echo of the boot sound that* Miguel *hears in his mind.)*

MIGUEL: NO! (Miguel *stomps into the ground in protest...and up comes a strain of* Kiki's *music.)*

JUDGE: What did you say, son? (Miguel *stomps again—more music.)*

MIGUEL: *(Amazed.)* Kiki...right through the ground, like a radio! You hear it?

JUDGE: *(Under his breath.)* Kid's loco... (Miguel *does a few steps of* Kiki's *dance.)*

MIGUEL: You heard it, didn't you? The music...

JUDGE: Nope.

MIGUEL: It followed me!

JUDGE: Uh, son...

MIGUEL: It flew over the border! You can't stop it, señor, it's right here—in my story! *(Beat.)* And my story's SPREADING! It's catching—¡sí! *(Pointing to a girl in the audience.)* She's got it señor—she's got my story—and she's got a BIG MOUTH! *(To her.)* Una Bocona, ¿verdad? *(To the Judge.)* She's going to tell it on the buses so it rides all over the city... She's going to tell it LOUD, so the ANGELS can hear it...and then... *(We hear the wind, and, in the wind...)*

LA LLORONA'S VOICE: ¡Ay, mis hiiiijos!... *(She laughs.)*

MIGUEL: My story's in the wind! *(Yearning.)* It's flying HOME, Mamá! It's in the plaza, and in the fields... It's in the Big Head of the Rich Man... It's in the arms of the Poor Man, Papá...and he's putting down his machete...and he's telling the Soldier, "NO MÁS!"... "No more!" *(Beat.)* And he's singing... *(He sings Luis's song, speaking a translation between each line of the song for the Angelenos.)*

Brazos para trabajar—
Arms to work, eh, Papá—

Corazón para amar—
And a heart to love—

Semillas para plantar—
Seeds to plant—

¡Esta voz para gritar!
But a voice to cry out..and sing...

The Chorus *comes on and sings with* Miguel.

ALL: *(Singing triumphantly.)*
    Canta verso a verso,
    y baila paso a paso,
    oye mi bocón—
    ¡el canto volará!

The Chorus *finishes with a rhythmic beating of sticks, and...*

CHORUS: Imagine this place—¡fíjate, imagine!

End of Play

El Chevy Azul (The Blue Chevy)

(To be sung by a child.)

They took my father last week
en el Chevy azul, en el Chevy azul,
and they hurt him bad,
saw them take my dad,
en el Chevy azul.

They took Francisco's son
in the Chevy azul, in the Chevy azul,
they were taking his aunt
and Poshis said they can't,
in the Chevy azul.

They hit her with their gun...
You're dead or on the run
from the Chevy azul.

They took Marta along
in the Chevy azul, in the Chevy azul,

she was singing a song,
and they said it was wrong,
in the Chevy azul.

They took my mother last night
in the Chevy azul,
I hope she'll be all right
in the Chevy azul.

They took my brothers, all three,
in the Chevy azul,
tonight they'll come for me…
in the Chevy azul.

One day I'll get me a car,
la la la la la la, la la la la la la,
and I'll drive it so far
la la la la la la…

And before the road ends,
pick up all my friends,
from the Chevy azul.

And They Come Here To Be Free

There is a land of laughter,
the jaguars dance, the birds soar,
the mist is green, the air is clean,
but the land is filled with war—
and they come here to be free.

There are soldiers in the forests,
and bombs in the trees,
the priests are in prison,
whole country's on its knees—

and they come here to be free.

Chorus:

They're our neighbors,
they're our brothers—
cross our borders
take our orders—
if they want to be free.

Machu Pichu, Quetzaltenango,
climb a mountain, dance a fandango,
to be free.

There is a land of laughter—
Why are the children crying?
They watch the rain fall, the corn grow tall...
and they watch their parents dying—
and they come here to be free.

Journey Song

My house got away from me—
whole village took off—
over that mountain,
back there—
I don't see it anywhere.

Se me perdió la casa,
mi pueblo se fue.

Fear is racing me—
I hear his feet,
I smell his sweat,
I feel his heat,
everywhere.

Y sólo el miedo me accompaña.

Tonight I'll sleep
in a strange place,
I won't know is name,
it won't be the same,
as my home.

Esta noche me acuesto
en cama extraña,
y sólo el miedo me accompaña.

Mañana me levanto
en cama extraña,
y sólo el miedo me accompaña.

Quetzal's Song

(The Quetzal is the Bird of Freedom.)

Mi tierra no tiene frontera,
ni jaulas para encerrar.
Está marcada por la risa
y los pasos del corazón.

Mi tierra no sabe "¡no canten!"
Mi tierra no entiende "no vuelen,"
todos hablamos un idioma,
y cantamos "libertad".

Y para llegar a mi tierra,
no necesitas dinero,
sólo las alas de la esperanza,
¡la locura de la esperanza
y la fe de una canción!

Allá no se come el odio,
tampoco bebemos miedo.
Sembramos semillas de paz,
que algún día han de crecer.

Y para llegar a mi tierra,
no necesitas permiso,
sólo las alas de la esperanza,
¡la locura de la esperanza,
y pluma de cualquier color!

English Verses:

My land, it has no cages,
My land, it has no borders,
My land is marked by laughter
and the footsteps of the heart.

And if you come to mi tierra,
you don't need a passport.
Just bring a song for my people,
a crazy song of hope for my people,
and wings — any color at all.

The Day They Stole All The Colors

by
Héctor Santiago

Translation and lyrics
by
Joe Rosenberg

To Emily for a Better World

The Day They Stole All the Colors
by Héctor Santiago

Characters

ACTOR
RENÉ (Earthling Boy)
CANELO (His Dog)
TINGO TILINGO (Ferocious Pirate)
TILINGO TINGO (Villainous Cowboy)
NEWS COMMENTATOR
2 OLD LADIES (Sell candies and toys on the
    street corner.)
STUDENT
TRAFFIC COP
PAINTER
3 MARTIANS (With Stilts)
KLAPKLIP (Martian Girl)
THREETHREE (Urano's Animal)
URANIANS (With Parasols)
DIONOS (Horse with Wings)
PLUTONIANS (With Glasses)

This play is conceived as a great visual spectacle, a game using the possibilities of children's theater: puppets, fright masks, marionettes, shadow puppets, black light, cine and so forth, For the purpose of inviting audience participation, each visual description in the dialogue can be accompanied by the theatrical effect it suggests. If an intermission is desired, it can be between scenes four and five, although ideally it is preferable not to break the rhythmic continuity of the play.

Prologue

Intergalactic music and lighting. The universe is described by the light show, with shooting stars, meteors, meteorites, and so forth. Actor, *dressed like a cosmonaut, enters.*

ACTOR: As you know, the Earth is not the only thing there is in space: there are thousands of stars, planets, suns that send out light to other worlds. Some are kind of near, others very far away. Outer Space is being studied so that we can know more about it. *(Confidentially.)* But there is one guy who is studying Outer Space for not such nice purposes. Years ago, long long ago, when there still were such things as pirates, there was one who was the most terrifying of them all... *(Shudders.)* Everybody called him Peg Leg, but his real name was Tingo Tilingo... *(Shudders.)* The most ferocious pirate of the Southern Seas! *(Enter* Tingo *on his ship, peering spying, through his telescope).* He was always

75

searching for valuable things, so that he could steal them! More than anything else, he loved to steal gold! One day as he was spying out on the horizon, he saw a tremendous light cross outer space: it was a comet. *(Comet dances in the sky.)* Now comets are purely rocks and ice travelling through space. But this comet was special, because it gave off a brilliant golden light which made it seem like a gigantic gold nugget. *(*Tingo *puts a hand behind an ear to listen.)* Did I say gold? *(*Tingo *sits.)* Did I say it seemed to be a gigantic ball of... *(*Tingo *rushes about, all over the place, desperately trying to figure out how he can trap the comet.)* Never say words like that near a pirate! Look what it has done to Tingo Tilingo!...He's going to try to capture the comet!... What do you think? Think he will? *(*Tingo *takes the anchor chain and circles it around his head. Then the comet passes near him. He throws the anchor and traps the comet, trying to haul it onto the boat. After a struggle the comet ascends and carries* Tingo, *holding on to the anchor, up with it.* Tingo *roars!* Actor laughs.)* Have any of you ever seen such a stupid pirate? And for what? For gold! Listen— Tingo Tilingo was hauled into space by the tail of that comet... *(Comet enters with* Tingo *holding on, disappears.)* There! Traveling all over outer space. But you know something? He wasn't all by himself very long...*(Shots. Music of the "Wild West.")* You see, that villainous cowboy, Tilingo Tingo, also thought the comet was made of gold.

(Enter Tilingo *with lasso.* Actor *shudders.)* He was the terror of the West!… In the afternoon he used to climb mountains to watch the passing of the comet. There was nobody like him when it came to lassos. And one day… *(Enter the comet with* Tingo. Tilingo *prepares his lasso and catches the comet. There is a struggle, and the comet hauls him up behind* Tingo. Actor *laughs.)* And so it happened that Tingo Tilingo and Tilingo Tingo got to know each other and they traveled through outer space where they got to know all about all the planets! That was when they conceived a diabolical plan to gain control of all the things that were important for all the planets. And I've got to tell you that they began by zeroing in on our planet, the Earth! That's where I begin our story by saying: Once upon a time there was a boy named René and Canelo, his dog… (Exits.)

Scene One

René's garden, full of smiling flowers, birds, and so forth. Enter Canelo, *barking behind birds and butterflies who escape him. Smells the flowers who laugh, tickled by his cold nose.* René *enters.*

RENÉ: Canelo! I told you to stop scaring the birds. This garden is for everyone, Leave the flowers along. *(Sun comes out.)* What a beautiful day! Let's water the flowers! *(He does and the flowers bathe happily.* Canelo *follows a caterpillar or bites a twig or gets wet by the hose, and so forth.*

A ladder falls from the sky, or some other effect: enter Tingo Tilingo *with his chain and anchor and* Tilingo Tingo *with his lasso. Music. A cloud hides the sun and darkness falls upon the garden.)*

TINGO TILINGO: From outer space we've come here in search of some new way to think up some entrapment to turn all people into slaves!

TINGO:
From the earthly planet
You just watch us!
All the colors, we'll take them all
They'll have to pay gold to us!

TILINGO:
And the stilts of the martians
All in our control
We'll be like their emperors
And we'll take away their gold!

BOTH:
And them Plutonian shades
We'll make them ours to ransom
And the Uranian parasols
Won't they make us look so handsome?
Tingo and Tilingo
Biggest crooks of all!
Tilingo and Tingo
Won't we be having a ball... *(Laugh.)*

TINGO: A garden! What a nice place to begin our work. Look at all them colors!

TILINGO: I can't wait to take them all away from here. And when we won't leave them with one single color... *(They laugh.)*

TINGO: We'll take something away from every planet. They'll all come to us to beg us to give them back what we capture, so we'll make them pay, and pay, and pay... Gold, gold, lots and lots of good old gold!

TILINGO: I'll be the best cowboy ever known in history! Tilingo Tingo, king of the lasso! King of the world!

TINGO: No, no... King of half the world...Is that clear?

TILINGO: *(Bothered.)* Sure, sure... Let's get to work! *(Twirls his lasso.)*

TINGO: What do you think you're doing?

TILINGO: I'm gonna rope them colors.

TINGO: Not if my name is Peg Leg, you don't! I'm the one who takes them colors, see? I'm a pretty ferocious pirate! *(They tangle angrily.)* Enough of this! Enough! *(Thinks.)* I'll give you... I'll give you the color of the...

TILINGO: The trees! (Tingo *negates with a shake of the head.)* The color of ice cream! (Tingo *disapproves again.)* The color of a flag! *(Same. Confused.)* I'll take them all away from you! This ain't my style... *(Considers.)* How are we gunna divide the loot? *(Happily.)* I got it! *(Surprises everybody by yanking some hairs out of* Tingo's *beard.)*

TINGO: What have you gone and done that for? Don't you know that for a pirate the most important things are his peg leg, the patch over his eye, and his beard? Those are the things that make me look terrifying. *(Makes a terrifying face to the kids in the audience.)*

TILINGO: The one who picks the shortest hair will be the one who captures the colors. *(*Tingo *takes one, turns away from* Tilingo, *hiding it, looks at it, smiles with satisfaction.* Tilingo *does the same.)* You first!

TINGO: You first! *(Carry on like this until each takes the other's hand and looks at the hair.)* I won! I won!

TILINGO: Please, Tingo: let me at least have yellow! I know you don't like yellow.

TINGO: But when I mix it with red I get orange!

TILINGO: Give me a break, Tingo Tilingo!

TINGO: I can't, Tilingo Tingo!

TILINGO: Tingo Tilingo!

TINGO: Tilingo Tingo!

TILINGO: Okay! But the stilts on Mars are for me!

BOTH:
Tingo and Tilingo
Biggest crooks of all!
Tilingo and Tingo
Won't we be having a ball!

(While Tingo *prepares his anchor to grab the colors, the cloud that obscured the sun, bares it so that light shines on the garden in all its splendor.* Canelo *chases after a cricket.* René *cleans the garden.* Canelo *sees a color go up and barks.)*

RENÉ: Why is that grass so pale? The heliotropes are losing their colors! The butterflies are all turning white! *(Watching a color disappear into the flies.)* The sky is all full of colors! And down here everything is turning white! *(Canelo runs out chasing after the last color.)* Canelo! Come back! Don' t chase the colors! You'll get lost, Canelo! *(Exits after* Canelo. *Blackout.)*

Scene Two

Large television screen. COMMENTATOR with microphone and behind him a Japanese landscape. Everything he says happens as he says it.

COMMENTATOR: The end of the world! The end of the world! We have to tell you what is happening to Japan! This morning all the fans turned white. The geishas' kimonos lost their color, nobody can tell anything from the tea leaves. Japan has turned entirely white! WHIIIIIITE! *(Blackout. Lights come up on an* Old Lady *who sells candies.)*

CANDY VENDOR: *(To kids.)* Candy! Candy! Who wants candy?... It's useless! Who wants to buy candy without knowing what flavor it is?... Green is for mint...red for strawberry, yellow for lemon... *(Sad.)* All I have is white candies. Even I don't know what flavor they are! Ever since the colors disappeared I haven't been able to sell a single candy! *(Enter* Toy Vendor *with her pinwheels, kites, beach balls, and so forth. It's all white.)*

TOY VENDOR: Sale! Sale! Pinwheels, kites, beach balls! Lots more! Cheap today! Today they're cheap! Come buy your kites! Here! Here! We also have a special on toys!... All over the town!

81

I've walked all over the town and my feet are killing me and nobody has bought a thing from me.

CANDY VENDOR: Who's going to want to buy things without color? Everything you have seems the same!

TOY VENDOR: *(Confidentially.)* I still have some with colors. *(*Tingo *overhears and prepares his grapple hook.)* In this box I have hidden some colored balls... They have brilliant colors! Look! I'll show them to you! *(As soon as she opens the box* Tingo *grabs the colors and runs.* Canelo *enters barking and exits in pursuit of* Tingo.*)* They were the only ones I had left! What am I going to be able to sell now? *(Enter* René.*)*

RENÉ: Has anyone seen a dog who is chasing colors?

CANDY VENDOR: He went that way... Behind my reds, greens and browns...

TOY VENDOR: My yellows, oranges and violets...

RENÉ: I'll try to find your colors. Don't be sad. But now I have to find Canelo. *(Exits.)*

CANDY VENDOR: *(Leaving sadly.)* Candy! Whiiiii-iiite candy!

TOY VENDOR: Kites that have no color! *(Blackout. Television screen.)*

COMMENTATOR: The same news comes to us from places all over the world! In Africa the zebras have all gone white, in Guatemala the feathers of the Quetzal bird have lost their color, in Holland the tulips have all turned white, in Mexico the jaguars no longer have spots, all over the world it's the same! The humming birds no longer have iridescent feathers. Turn to this station for latest developments. *(Blackout.)*

Scene Three

A park. Each character enclosed in his own problems. A Student is surrounded by opened books that are all white, There is only one closed. He looks at some of them and becomes discouraged.

STUDENT: How am I going to study with books that have lost their letters? White books without any drawings even! No photos, no maps, no chapter headings!... I'll never make it through school! *(Taking one up.)* And this is the last book, the only one I have not opened and found!... I don't dare open it, even! If the colors run out of it? *(Automobile horns. A desperate* Policeman *tries to regulate traffic, watches with bewilderment as the colors of the traffic lights leave up into the sky.)*

POLICEMAN: Nobody knows when to stop or go or let the pedestrians cross! With the colors of the lights disappeared, traffic is paralyzed! I've never seen anything like this! A whole city without any colors! *(A* Painter *with his tubes of paint, his palette and his brush tries to paint the flowers, the fountain, and so forth. But the colors rise up and disappear into the sky.)*

PAINTER: This is useless! I come here expecting the park to be as it always is. Now the children don' t even want to come here to play! And my poor paintings! How can you possibly expect to paint a totally colorless universe? Goodbye art! *(All complain at the same time. Enter* René.*)*

RENÉ: Has anyone seen a dog chasing after colors?

STUDENT: Shut up! *(Everybody is suddenly quiet.)* This is the last book that still has colors! Maybe if I open it very slowly... Very slowly! *(Everyone surrounds him with bated breath. Very carefully.)* Like this. A little...a little... *(Offstage* Canelo *barks, startling him, causing him to open the book quickly. The alphabet starts to rise up to the sky. Enter* Canelo *and he bites a letter as it rises, does not let it go. He rises with the letter.* René *grabs the last letter and rises up into the flies with it.)*

POLICEMAN: Stop that! Come down now!

RENÉ: I'm going to see who's stealing all the colors. I promise to return and bring all the colors back to the Earth. Adioooós! *(Disappears.Commotion down below.* Tingo *and* Tilingo, *their hands full of colors, laugh their fool heads off. Those down below look at them sadly and then disappear. Blackout. A view of the universe. Light on the* Commentator *without television screen.)*

COMMENTATOR: Yes, my friends. It is confirmed that a boy named René and his dog, Canelo, have gone off into outer space to look for the lost colors. A bulletin from Russia confirms that an evil pirate was seen stealing the colors. In Hawaii a villainous cowboy was observed doing the same thing. We have no knowledge at this moment as to the identity of these criminals or why they have stolen the colors. It is very possible that our friends, René and his cherished dog, Canelo, are in imminent danger. *(Looks up into the firmament.)* We can do nothing because they have left Earth! Stay tuned for the latest developments. *(Blackout.)*

Scene Four

Mars, a red planet full of canals consisting of sand. Music. Enter Martians mounted on stilts. They do the dance of the stilts.

MARTIANS:
>There only is one sun
>But on Mars we have moons aplenty
>This old planet is fiery red
>Red as a ripe tomato.
>The canals of this planet
>Are of sand we keep squeeky white
>To walk our stilts upon them
>Without them 'twould be such a fright!
>Our stilts would bend out of shape
>Blisters on our feet
>They're worth more than all the gold mines
>And the pearls of the ocean deep.

(Off stage laughter of Tingo *and* Tilingo. *Then a scream and weeping.)*

MARTIAN 1: What's happening, Klap?

M2: Don't know, Klep. Do you know, Klip?

M3: *(Motioning off.)* Those are Klop and Klup. They don't have their stilts. *(Sympathize.)*

M1: That has never happened before! Has it, Klap, Klip?

M2: It's like Klep says. What do you think, Klip, shouldn't we help Klop and Klup? Klep?

M3: Let's go Klap, Klep. *(Shouts.)* Take it easy, Klop and Klup. Klap, Klep and Klip are on their way to help you out. *(Confusion. Nobody knows where to exit and they fall all over one another. Finally* M3 *gets to the exit.)* Klap and Klep! *(They follow him. Enter* Tingo *and* Tilingo *on stilts.* Tilingo *carries the stolen stilts which are wrapped up in his lasso.)*

TILINGO: See how important stilts are? Martians need them for everything! Without them they can't move, or clean their canals, and when the sun is strong... *(Laughs.)* We will be the rulers of all Mars! Look! What more do we need? We're going to rake it all in! (Tingo peers through his telescope.)

TINGO: I don' t believe this! You remember that stupid old mutt that was chasing after us?

TILINGO: Him, and his master too!

TILINGO: They're still following us!... If they find us everyone will know that it was we who stole the colors on Planet Earth...

TILINGO: And the stilts on Planet Mars. What are we gunna do? *(They pace, get an idea, dismiss it, bump into each other and are just about to fall down.)* I've got it! *(Conspiratorially.)* We'll make it look like they are the ones who stole the colors—and the stilts too! The Martians will want to lynch them. And while they try to explain their innocence... We take off for the parasols of Planet Uranus. *(They hug each other happily.)*

TINGO: You're very intelligent for a cowboy!

TILINGO: And you... A peg leg!... *(Exeunt laughing.)*

RENÉ: *(Off stage.)* Let's get off here, Canelo. Watch out! We're there. Let go of those letters... Now, Canelo! *(They fall on stage.)* Where are we? You're all covered up with sand. *(Shakes* Canelo.*)* This place looks like one big desert. *(Looks around.)* Wherever I turn all I see is rocks and sand! (Canelo *goes to some rocks sheltered from the brilliant rays of the sun. He barks.)* What a fine place you've found! *(Goes there and falls asleep.* Canelo *hears the Martians and exits, following them. Enter stealthily* Tingo *and* Tilingo. *They lay some stilts down alongside the sleeping* René. *Smiling happily they hide behind the rocks. Enter* Canelo *followed by the Martians.)*

M1: What is that, Klap?

M2: Don't know, Klep. You know, Klip?

M3: Klap and Klep, have you ever in your life seen anything that hairy?

M1: And look, Klap and Klip—what tusks it has!

M2: Don't forget, Klep and Klip, it has four feet! Let's capture it! *(They try in vain.* Canelo *wakes* René *with his barking.)*

RENÉ: What's going on? *(The* Martians *stop and look at him surprised.)*

M3: Klap and Klep, that's a rare creature! What can it be?

RENÉ: Where am I?

M1: On the Planet Mars. I am Klep, this is Klap and this Klip.

RENÉ: Pleased to meet you, Klap, Klep, Klup. I come from the Planet Earth and my name is René—just plain René, and this is my dog, Canelo.

M2: Have you seen our stilts?

RENÉ: I just arrived on Mars. All I've seen is sand, sand and more sand.

M1: Our people say they were stolen by some men who look real strange. *(Looks at him suspiciously.)*

M1: *(Similarly.)* Two strangers!

M2: *(Similarly.)* Possibly Earthlings. (Tingo *and* Tilingo *laugh, self satisfied.* Canelo *barks at them and they flee off stage. The* Martians *see the stilts.)* Klep, Klip! There are our stilts!

M3: You said you knew nothing about them. You're a liar! You have lied to Klap, Klep and Klip.

M1: You're a crook! *(Uselessly* René *tries to explain, but the* Martians *surround him with anger.* Canelo *barks at them.* René *follows suit, and all leave, followed by the angry* Martians. *On the ladder* Tingo *and* Tilingo *with the stolen stilts.)*

TINGO: Just like we planned!

TILINGO: Now we take possession of Mars!

TINGO: Then to Planet Uranius, the yellow planet!

BOTH:
Tingo and Tilingo
Biggest crooks of all!
Tilingo and Tingo
Won't we be having some ball!

*(They leave. Flowers made of redish rock bloom.
Enter KLAPKLIP, very sad.)*

KLAPKLIP: Where are my stilts? While I was picking these colored rocks someone stole them.
Where can I go without them? On Mars nobody
knows how to do anything without stilts.
(Canelo, off stage, barks. She is frightened.)
What is that? *(Looks off stage.)* What strange
creatures! And they're coming this way! *(Hides
behind her flowers. Enter* René *on stilts, followed by* Canelo.)*

RENÉ: How am I going to convince them that we
haven't stolen their stilts? They're furious with
us! They haven't caught up with us because they
don't know how to run without stilts, but they'll
be here any minute. And we don't know where
we can hide. *(Canelo barks in the direction of the
cave of Klapklip.)* What, Canelo? *(Canelo goes to
Klapklip who comes out, frightened and stumbles over René, both falling to the ground. Klapklip is cornered by Canelo.)* Don't be afraid;
Canelo won't hurt you. Come here, Canelo.
Aren't there any dogs on Mars? *(She negates.)*
Where we come from there are lots of them.
(The planet Earth turns blue.) I come from
there, from Planet Earth, My name is René. And
yours?

KLAPKLIP: My name is Klapklip, and I pick rocks.

RENÉ: Oh. Why do you pick rocks?

KLAPKLIP: Many years ago we had lots of trees
and flowers. But everyone polluted the water
and wasted it. They treated the land just as

badly, so that it all turned into sand. Since then we never had trees and flowers. So we made some out of rocks. *(Shows them.)* They don't smell but this way we don't forget that in other places flowers still exist. *(Sadly.)* Someone stole my stilts.

RENÉ: Maybe it was the ones I came across in the middle of the desert. *(Shows them.)*

KLAPKLIP: All the stilts have the owners names on them to keep from getting mixed up.

RENÉ: *(Reads the name on his stilts.)* Klopklop. And your name is Klapklip... I'm sorry!... But I swear to you I'll catch the scoundrels! They won't be robbing people very long, if I can help it!

KLAPKLIP: What's that word mean? Robbing.

RENÉ: Taking what doesn't belong to you without permission.

KLAPKLIP: On Mars we do not have that word. Here everything has the name of the owner written on it. Even the flowers. (Reads) Klap, Klep, Klip, Klop, Klup...

RENÉ: (Looking off) Klap, Klep, Klip, Klop, Klup! Here they come! They think we're the ones who stole their stilts. If they catch us we won't be able to catch the real thieves.

KLAPKLIP: That could be very dangerous. They are probably very bad people. You need help. *(Picks up the basket.)* Here are some things that can help you out.

RENÉ: Thanks, Klapklip, but we haven't any time to lose...

KIAPKLIP: I could help you. After all, they stole my stilts too.

RENÉ: Explain that to Klap, Klep, Klip, Klop and Klup. Tell them we're not the thieves. We're going to get their stilts back for them. Come on, Canelo! *(Puts the stilts on the ground. As he does* Tilingo *lassoes him and they start to go up into the sky.* René *takes hold of* Canelo. Klapklip, *basket in hand, takes hold of the other stilt, and she rises into the sky.)* You have to stay there! Don't, Klapklip!

KLAPKLIP: I'm coming along to help you! We'll be three against those villains! *(Enter the* Martians *who look at them amazed.)* Adiós, Klap, Klep, Klip, Klop, Klup! Adiós! *(Disappear. Blackout on the bewildered Martians.)*

Scene Five

Uranus, the yellow planet. If black light is available, a dance of parasols of all shapes painted in a range of phosphorescent colors. The dance over, RENÉ, KLAPKLIP, and CANELO come tumbling down from the sky.

RENÉ: Where are we? *(Enter* Threethree, *an animal with a kangaroo pouch. He wears a parasol on his head as if it were a hat. Everything he finds he puts in his pouch.)*

THREETHREE: In Uranus! One, welcome. Two, my name is Threethree. And three, who are you? And four, what are you doing on Uranus?

KLAPKLIP: My name is Klapklip and...

THREETHREE: One, no; two no; and three no! Here on Uranus everything has a number. Therefore you have to say: "One, my name is! Klapklip; two..." Got it? *(They look at him in amazement.)*

KLAPKLIP: *(Timidly.)* One, my name is Klapklip; two I come from the Planet Mars; three, this is René from the Planet Earth; four, this is his dog, Canelo; five, we're chasing after crooks; six, to get back what was stolen from the rightful owners; seven, and make the crooks pay for their crimes; eight, we think they took off for Uranus; nine, tell us if they stole anything here from you; and ten, watch out, everyone!

THREETHREE: Eleven, I can help you; twelve, I am simply a Uranian Threethree; thirteen, the real Uranians are the ones you see coming here, wearing their parasols.

RENÉ: Fourteen, why does everyone around here carry a parasol?

THREETHREE: Fifteen, they'll tell you. *(Enter Uranians.)*

U1: Sixteen, who are you?

RENÉ: Seventeen, René from the Planet Earth; eighteen, my dog, Canelo; nineteen Klapklip from the Planet Mars.

THREETHREE: Twenty, they're searching for some crooks; and twenty-one, they want to know why everyone on Uranus carries parasols. *(Uranians look at one another perplexed.)*

U2: Twenty-two, nobody has ever asked us that question before; twenty-three, the truth is we don't know; twenty-four, our fathers and our grandfathers and our forefathers used them, and... *(Tingo and Tilingo, disguised as magicians carrying a grapple iron and a lasso, appear. Making a display of secrecy, they listen eagerly to all of it.)*

URANIANS: Twenty-five, we work all day under the parasols; twenty-six, we live all day under the parasols; twenty-seven, we spend our lives taking care of our parasols; twenty-eight, we argue about which parasol is the prettiest one; twenty-nine, we invent all different kinds of parasols; *(Showing them off, amused.)* parasols with pockets, parasols with pointed peaks, parasols with flounces, parasols with music...

TINGO: I knew it! The most important thing on Uranus are the parasols!

KLAPKLIP: Okay, okay...what number are we at? *(René counts with his fingers.)* Thirty, but why use them if you don't know why? *(Uranians have a noisy meeting in which everyone tries to talk at the same time, look at Klapklip, René and Canelo and shrug.)*

RENÉ: Thirty-one, let's go take a look if we can see anything out there.

THREETHREE: Thirty-two, I'm going with you. *(They leave.)*

TILINGO: The field is clear for us! Don't forget our plan. Nobody gets in the way, we take all the parasols! *(Magician music. Cloud of smoke.)*

TINGO: Thirty-three, the magicians have arrived on Uranus! Thirty-four, the most famous magicians in all the universe! Thirty-five, experts in making things disappear and reappear! Thirty-six, we are the Great Abu and the great Baba! Thirty-seven, acclaimed throughout all the planets! *(Waits for* Tilingo. *Kicks him in the butt.)*

TILINGO: *(Hiding behind a smile as he massages his butt.)* Thirty-eight, we have come here to Uranus to demonstrate something you have never seen; thirty-nine, the things you have lost under your parasols, Forty, we will execute the great magical effect of the lasso to make all the parasols disappear. *(*Uranians *murmur uneasily.)* Forty-one, don't worry, we always return what we make disappear. *(Relief.)* Forty-two, let us begin! *(Drum roll. Lasso work. As each parasol disappears, the owner takes shelter with his neighbor. Now only three parasols are left, with the Uranians crowded under them.)* Forty-three, the one before the last! Forty-four, the last!

URANIANS: Forty-five, please give them back right away, we don't know how to live without them.

TILINGO: Forty-six, we know that! And forty-seven, the last one! *(The Uranians cover their eyes and form a circle to protect themselves from the open daylight.)*

TINGO: Forty-eight, all done! Now let's go after the shades of Planet Pluto!

BOTH:
If something needs to be done right
Whether it be here or there

Take charge of it now
And you'll be in charge everywhere.

(Take off with laughter, leaving the poor Urani-ans *to shiver.* Canelo *enters and barks up at them in the sky. Enter* René, Klapklip *and* Threethree.*)*

THREETHREE: Forty-nine, we've arrived too late.

URANIANS: Fifty; we don't know what to do without our parasols. Fifty-one, they tell us that the light will harm us and the landscape is very ugly.

KLAPKLIP: Fifty-two, how are you going to know that if you never tried it? Fifty-three, open your eyes and you'll see it isn't that way at all!

URANIANS: Fifty-four, we're scared to!

RENÉ: Fifty-five, Threethree, take off your parasol. *(Fearfully* Threethree *does and looks at the daylight, sees that nothing happens to him, looks all around marvelling.)*

THREETHREE: Fifty-six, It's true! The sunlight isn't hurting me at all! and Uranus is a beautiful place!

URANIANS: Fifty-seven, don't pull our legs! *(*Klapklip *and* René *gently remove the hands of the* Uranians *from covering their eyes.* Uranians *look with a timidity that turns into happiness.)* Fifty-eight, we don t need our parasols!

RENÉ: Fifty-nine, what you need are some simple sunglasses.

U1: Sixty, sunglasses! Sixty-one, the magicians said they were going to take the glasses away from the Plutonians. *(General surprise. The lasso comes down from the sky and takes the sombrero of* Threethree, Klapklip *takes* Canelo *and grabs the rope.* René *and* Threethree *follow, disappear into the sky.)*

THEY: Sixty-two, hasta luego! *(Uranians below cheer them on, then turn to the public happily.)*

URANIANS:

Parasols gone, gone Parasols gone, gone

The whole world, I can see,

And enjoy the beautiful sunlight

And learn what it means to be free.

Blackout.

Scene Six

Pluto, the planet of the rains and perpetual snows where all the landscape is white. We hear the neighing of a horse. Enter the Dionos, *a white horse with wings and triangular shaped markings. It rests under a square tree: everything on Pluto is geometrical in form. Enter* Plutonians *engaged in desperate search, each wearing a different geometric emblem on his chest. They become discouraged, give up the search. See the public.*

P1: Have you seen any shades like these around here? *(Shows emblem.)* They were a beautiful pair of triangular shades. We need them so that the constant rains won't fall in our eyes, Without them we don't know what to do. It would be a great disaster for all Pluto. Who would want to take our shades? *(Enter other* Plutonians.*)* They don't know anything either.

P2: Maybe they've seen mine... *(To the kids, showing his emblem.)* They were square shades...

P3: Mine were rectangular...

P1: There were also round ones, and pentagonal... It makes me sad just to think about this! *(They put their arms around one another, seeking and giving solace.)*

PLUTONIANS: What are we going to do without our shades? *(Leave in tears. Enter* René, Canelo, Klapklip *and* Threethree.*)*

RENÉ: Someone's crying...

DIONOS: Because someone has stolen all the shades in Uranus.

KLAPKLIP: We got here too late.

THREETHREE: One, what do we do now? Two, because this is the last of the planets.

DIONOS: How strange the way you talk! Who are you?

THREETHREE: Three, my name is Threethree and I come from the Planet Uranus.

RENÉ: I'm René from the Planet Earth, and this is my dog, Canelo. *(Canelo barks.)*

KLAPKLIP: I am Klapklip from the Planet Mars.

DIONOS: I'm one of the Dioni of Pluto. *(Neighs.)*

RENÉ: You look like a horse. The only thing is that the ones on Planet Earth don't have wings or those triangular marks on their bodies.

DIONOS: It's that everything here has a form... Rocks are round, trees square, clouds triangular...

THREETHREE: Four, you know something we don't about who stole the shades?

DIONOS: Well, I did see a comet that was loaded down with lots of things.

RENÉ: With colors? *(Dionos nods.)*

KLAPKLIP: With stilts? *(Same.)*

THREETHREE: Five, with parasols? *(Same.)*

DIONOS: And I have a feeling with our shades too. *(Enter Plutonians.)*

PLUTONIANS: Our shades?

RENÉ: They're some crooks who go around stealing things from all the planets.

KLAPKLIP: They want to take charge of the whole universe; become rich and powerful.

PLUTONIANS: Then good-bye to our shades forever? When the rains come we won't be able to see anything...

THRREETHREE: Six, and we're the ones who are hoping to catch them. We won't be able to though, even though there are many of us.

RENÉ: If we unite we can beat them, Right now the most important thing is to know where they're hiding.

DIONOS: I know, The comet looked very suspicious to me so I flew behind it for a while. I know where they landed.

KLAPKLIP: Yeah, and how do we get there?

DIONOS: I'll take you there. *(Happy, happy.)* You'll have to hold on to me real tight, because it's far away from here—a long trip.

PLUTONIANS: Will they give us back our shades?

RENÉ: If we all cooperate with one another, I'm sure you'll get your shades back.

All mount Dionos, *who starts to fly. Below, the* Plutonians *send them off happily. Blackout.*

Scene Seven

The Planet Saturn. It's rings are full of the stolen things. Everywhere are signs: "NO TRES-PASSING." "PRIVATE PROPERTY." "DON'T TOUCH ON PENALTY OF DEATH." "PROPERTY OF TINGO TILINGO." "PROPERTY OF TILINGO TINGO," and so forth. Enter RENÉ, CANELO, KLAPKLIP, THREETHREE *and* DIONOS.

THREETHREE: Four, look at that, will you! The colors, the stilts, the parasols, the shades!

KLAPKLIP: They've converted the Planet Saturn into a planet full of stolen goods! Those crooks! We never would have found them here if Dionos hadn't followed them!

RENÉ: We've got to be very careful now. They're probably nearby somewhere.

DIONOS: We can take all those things and hoof it before they get back. But we'll have to be super careful. *(The* Group *goes towards the stolen goods.)*

KLAPKLIP: Wait! Here's a sign!: "All who enter here will be put in jail" It's a trap! *(Canelo barks at* Tingo *and* Tilingo *who are hidden and trap them with the lasso and a net.* Canelo *escapes.)*

TINGO: Do they think they're smarter than Tingo Tilingo and Tilingo Tingo? We took precautions just in case they nosed around here. See how they're going to have to pay for following us and opposing our plans?

TILINGO: In order for each planet to get back what we liberated from it, they'll have to name us governors and give us all the riches they have! We'll be the rulers of it all!

BOTH: *(Dancing.)*
Tingo and Tilingo
biggest crooks of all!
Tilingo and Tingo
Won't we be having some ball!

RENÉ: They won't get away with this! They'll have to return all they've stolen!

KLAPLIP: And they'll be punished for it! THEY WILL!

BOTH: I m scared!

THREETHREE: Six, we'll defeat them because we're united.

TINGO: How can they be united when they're all so different? And each one of them comes from somewhere else. Not one of them is anything like the other.

DIONOS: That won't stop us from uniting to fight you! We may look different, but we are equal!

RENÉ: And we respect one another as we are!

TINGO: Well, me too, I accept pirates like myself...

TILINGO: And me cowboys like myself...

KLAPKLIP: But there are all different kinds of people in the world. You don't have to hate people just because they aren't like you—you crooked bums!

TILINGO: Enough of that! We're very busy right now counting all our riches. What should we do with them, Tingo Tilingo? *(Pace, musing, collide, and so forth.)*

KLAPPKLIP: I have a plan! *(Talk secretly among themselves.)*

TINGO: I know! Let' s find the anchor! We'll catch the comet again and put them on it all tied up!

TILINGO: And they'll go all over the universe like us! What an intelligent Peg Leg you are! Now they'll know what it's like to travel all over outer space forever. Nobody will be able to save them! Let's look for the anchor!

KLAPKLIP: Just a minute. If you let me loose, I'll show you the diamond mines on Mars, the ones where the red diamonds are!

TINGO: I've never seen red diamonds.

KLAPKLIP: Look in my basket. *(Go to the basket and find some real stones which fill the place with bright light.)*

TILINGO: They re mine!

TINGO: They're mine! *(Argue and fight.)*

KLAPKLIP: On Mars there's enough for both of you! Mountains of diamonds!

BOTH: Where? How do we get there? What part of Mars?

KLAPKLIP: I'm the only one who knows. I can take you there if you let me loose. *(T&T hold a conference about it.)*

TINGO: All right. You'll came with us. But those others go on the comet.

TILINGO: *(To the kids.)* And when we have all the diamonds, we'll put her on the comet too. *(Free* Klapklip, *and while they retie the net she goes off to one side.)*

KLAPKLIP: *(Laughing.)* Tingo Tilingo and Tilingo Tingo! *(Gives them a sign to follow her out, which they do, roaring. Enter* Canelo.*)*

RENÉ: Untie these knots, Canelo. *(*Canelo *does.)*

DIONOS: What do we do now? We've got to think of something while Klapklip still leads them on.

RENÉ: We have to find a way to trap them.

THREETHREE: Seven, I know how to help you. (Takes all kinds of junk out of his pouch, even fruit.) Eight, this is a fruit from Uranus called Nine-Ten. It's odor is so strong it knocks out whoever sniffs it. I'll leave it here so they find it. We'll make believe we're still tied up.

DIONOS: They trapped Klapklip! Back to the net! *(Do so. Enter* Tilingo *with chain and anchor.* Tingo *pushes* Klapklip *in.)*

TINGO: For fooling us, it's to the comet with you, just like them! We'll find out how to get hold of the diamonds on Mars.

THREETHREE: Nine, but you won't find Nine-Ten, the fruit of gold.

BOTH: The fruit of gold?

THREETHREE: Ten, there's one of them. It's the fruit that has gold nuggets for seeds. The trees are full of Nine-Ten, all over the place, full of gold, gold, gold... (Tingo *grabs at the fruit, but* Tilingo *does too. They fight, then part.*)

RENÉ: Beat it, Klapklip! (T&T *become enveloped in a smoke which paralyzes them. The* Others *come out from under the net, and tie* T&T *up in it.*)

DIONOS: WE'VE WON (*They go to the stolen goods.*) The shades of Pluto.

THREETHREE: The uranian parasols!

KLAPKLIP: The Martian stilts! (Looks at René.) Why don't you take the colors?

RENÉ: I've been thinking that since Mars is all red, maybe they could use a little of our colors.

KLAPKLIP: And I will be able to give some stilts with which the children can play...

THREETHREE: Maybe the Plutonian shades would be better for the sun...

DIONOS: And the parasols for the rain! (*General glee. Tricks.*)

RENÉ: Now each of us returns to his planet. We'll see what punishment is fit for those crooks. (*To the kids.*) Y colorín colorado, el cuento se está acabando! (*Blackout.*)

Final Scene

A light on the Commentator.

COMMENTATOR: Our latest information has been confirmed that a rain of parasols fell on Planet Pluto, a rain of shades on Planet Uranus, a rain of colors on Mars, and here on Planet Earth it's raining stilts! It is said that the thieves Tingo Tilingo and Tilingo Tingo have been brought to

Planet Earth to receive their punishment. We'll keep you informed of developments. *(Light on* Plutonians *with parasols,* Uranians *with shades,* Martians *with colors and* Earthlings *with stilts. Comet passes by. All salute it.* Dionos, Threethree, Klapklip, *and* René *take places.)*

RENÉ: Thanks, Klapklip, Threethree and Dionos. *(*Canelo *barks)* Thanks, Canelo! *(All thank one another. Enter* Tingo Tilingo *and* Tilingo Tingo *in prison uniforms, dragging ball and chain. They sweep the floor as they pass. Music. Everyone dances.)*

ALL:
United, united, united
All of who are the same
And are different
As one together
Will overcome!

RENÉ: And now, good friends...

ALL: Colorín colorado, este cuento se ha terminado!

The Legend of the Golden Coffee Bean

by

Manuel Martín, Jr.

A One-Act Play with Music

The Legend of the Golden Coffee Bean
by Manuel Martín, Jr.

Note to the Reader

The Legend of the Golden Coffee Bean *was espe-cially written for children attending elementary school. Although I avoided the direct didactic treat-ment of this imaginary trip through Central Amer-ica, some of the terms and situations are meant to "teach" the children as an audience. Some of the dif-ficult terms like "exportation" are meant to be clari-fied by the director of the play and the actors. Improvisations are welcome for the purpose of clari-fication. If at the end of the play there are still geo-graphical, historical, cultural or sociological questions, the teachers, actors and director, should be on hand for answers and further explanations.*

Characters

CHOMIHA
NARRATOR
GUCUMATZ

SUNFLOWER
IQUI BALAM
OLD MAN
COY
TEACHER
QUEL
VAC
YAK

All the above characters, with the exception of Chomiha, are to be played by a single actor/musician/dancer. Voice changes and the use of masks could be helpful for the development of the characters.

Chomiha *an Indian girl about ten, appears center stage. She moves downstage towards the stage's edge, then she kneels and covers her eyes with her hands.*

NARRATOR: Hi! I'm the narrator of this play... I'm going to tell you the magical and wonderful story of the Golden Coffee Bean! It's the story of Chomiha's journey into the many lands of Central America. Chomiha is a homeless Indian girl who was born near the borders of Belize and Guatemala, in Central America. *(Pause.)* Chomiha is a Maya. Have you heard about the Mayan people? *(Period of questions and answers.)* Yes, some of you do...some of you don't...Well, the Mayas live in Central America. Do you know where Central America is located? *(Period of questions and answers.)* Do you know

how many countries are in Central America? Do
you know the name of those countries? *(Period
of questions and answers.)* Right! Chomiha is a
descendant of the Mayas. That means that her
grand-mother was a Maya, her great-great-
grand mother was a Maya too... You should
know, children, that the Mayas were a very civilized people long before Columbus discovered
the Americas. Yes, yes, they were a cool, happy
people. They had great cities, they built roads
out of stones, constructed large pyramids to
worship their Gods... and were also great
artists. You should see some of the wonders they
invented: golden statues and jewelry, colorful
wall paintings similar to those found in Egypt,
great palaces and temples, and many pyramids
all over the magical land of Central America.
They were also the greatest astronomers of the
world. They explored the skies with large tele-
scopes searching for other civilizations beyond
the horizon...they created the most accurate calendar of the globe, which we still use today.
They had a very complex and civilized society.
Yes, the empire of the Mayas—the oldest civi-
lization of the Americas—collapsed before the
Spanish conquest in the sixteenth century. But
the Mayan language is still spoken by one and a
half million people in Central America. Yes,
Central America has a green, green jungle, and
this jungle is full of animals...snakes, mon-
keys...parrots...wild birds and wild huge volcanoes!... And do you know what's wrong with

volcanoes, don't you?... ERUPTIONS!... TREMORS!... QUAKES!... EARTHQUAKES!... EARTHQUAKES!!! *(The* Narrator *exits. The sound of an erupting volcano is heard over the loudspeakers.)*

CHOMIHA: *(To the audience.)* I am weeping to relieve my sadness. My tears join the current of this river. *(She makes ritualistic sounds of weeping.* Gucumatz *enters.)*

GUCUMATZ: Chomiha, why are you crying? *(*Chomiha *keeps crying.)* Stop weeping, unless you want to overflow the river. *(Pause.)* I'm Gucumatz.

CHOMIHA: I'm Chomiha, which in the language of the Quiché Indians means "Beautiful and Chosen Water." *(She keeps weeping.)*

GUCUMATZ: Stop crying! *(Pause.)* You did not answer my question.

CHOMIHA: I've lost everything I loved in an earthquake... My parents, my two little brothers, my friends, my whole village... All buried when our homes collapsed. I was left alone... An orphan...

GUCUMATZ: Chomiha, I understand your grief. But you are a descendant of the Mayas. Your people have survived worse disasters. *(Pause.)* They even survived the Spaniards...

CHOMIHA: *(Stops weeping and gets up.)* It's easy for you to say. What am I going to do? I am alone and unprotected.

GUCUMATZ: Perhaps I can help you.

CHOMIHA: Can you? Would you show me the way to become rich and have it easy?

GUCUMATZ: Well…*(After a long pause.)* Perhaps I can share a secret with you… You said you wanted to be wealthy.

CHOMIHA: Yes.

GUCUMATZ: Well, I can tell you where to find a golden coffee bean. This bean possesses magic qualities. Once this bean is planted, a coffee plant will sprout and grow in seconds, and millions of golden beans will appear. Isn't that easy? You'll be the wealthiest girl in the world!

CHOMIHA: How can I find the golden coffee bean?

GUCUMATZ: Wait! There is only one condition. I won't give you any instructions unless you bring me pure water from a river in the unexplored lands of Belize.

CHOMIHA: Belize. I know the way. *(Searches around the stage and finally finds a bucket.)* Will you wait for me here?

GUCUMATZ: Yes, I will.

CHOMIHA: I'll be back in no time at all.

GUCUMATZ: *(Laughing.)* Have a nice journey! (Chomiha *runs in circles almost in ritual-like leaps. After a short time, She stops to mop her brow.)*

CHOMIHA: Oh, I'm so tired and hungry. *(A huge sunflower descends next to* Chomiha.*)* My God! I never realized you were there. I love sunflower seeds. (Chomiha *tries to remove seeds from some of the dried flowers.)*

SUNFLOWER: Stop!

CHOMIHA: I've never heard a sunflower speak.

SUNFLOWER: I've never met a girl so fresh! I won't let you use my seeds unless you give me something.

CHOMIHA: *(To the audience.)* It seems that in life you can't get anything for nothing. *(To the* Sunflower *as she walks away.)* I'm very poor, so I guess I better be on my way...

SUNFLOWER: Come back! I didn't mean that you've got to pay me with money.

CHOMIHA: What else could I give you?

SUNFLOWER: Think!...

CHOMIHA: Perhaps if I sing you a song.

SUNFLOWER: Well, if I like it...

CHOMIHA: It's a song about sunflowers. The song goes: "Meet the sunflower, queen of them all."

SUNFLOWER: *(In a grand manner.)* I think I already like it.

CHOMIHA: *(Sings.)*
King of the planets
Luminous sun
Meet the sunflower
Queen of them all

Petal by petal
Smiling at you
King of the planets
She is embracing you

High in the skies
You are her warmest friend
She's the tallest flower
The brightest of all

Meet your lovely mate
Oh, luminous king
Admire your reflection
Now you found your queen

Your queen is the sunflower
She's queen of them all

(After she finishes the song.) Did you like it?

SUNFLOWER: Of course I did. *(Pause.)* You may take all my seeds.

CHOMIHA: (Begins to remove all of the dried seeds and deposits them in her burlap bag.) Thank you, thank you! *(Chomiha runs in circles again using her dance-like ritualistic leaps. SHE stops downstage in front of the orchestra pit, bends forward and lowers the bucket.)*

CHOMIHA: This river seems to have pure water.

NARRATOR: Belize was once a British colony. That's why it was the only country in Central America where English was spoken. But now, Belize is independent.

CHOMIHA: No wonder this water is crystal clear. *(She lifts the bucket and runs in circles using the dance-like movements again. She stops center stage and looks up, searching for Gucumatz. She calls.)* Gucumatz! Gucumatz!

GUCUMATZ: I'm here! My God you are fast!

CHOMIHA: Here is your pure water from Belize. Now, how can I get the Golden Coffee Bean?

GUCUMATZ: Well, it's simple. You must go to the town of Sonsonate, find a wise man by the name of Iqui Balam and then he will give you the Golden Coffee Bean.

CHOMIHA: That's easy! Good...

GUCUMATZ: *(Interrupts* Chomiha.*)* Wait! There is another condition.

CHOMIHA: *(To the audience.)* I knew it was coming...

GUCUMATZ: You must bring a *huipil* to Iqui Balam. *(A* huipil *attached to invisible wire descends center stage.)* The *huipil* should match the beauty of this one, but must be woven with your own hands.

CHOMIHA: Gee! But I don't know how to weave.... I don't! I don't! I don't! *(*Chomiha *throws a tantrum and begins to jump and kick in the air.)*

GUCUMATZ: Shame on you! You are in Guatemala, the land of the best Indian weavers and you don't know how to weave. Go and find someone to teach you.

CHOMIHA: But... Gucumatz.

GUCUMATZ: Call me when the *huipil* is finished.

NARRATOR: This is how Chomiha learns to weave a *huipil*. Chomiha meets Puhuy a wise Quiche Indian woman—Puhuy means owl—and begs her to teach her the mystery of weaving. While Puhuy shows Chomiha how to weave the colorful patterns, she tells about her Mayan ancestors and their struggle against the Spanish conquistadors. Chomiha learns not only to weave but about her own Mayan history. *(*Chomiha *moves center stage and takes the weaving tools out of a basket. She squats on the* *floor and slowly begins to work with the yarn. Lights fade out on* Chomiha *while she weaves a small portion of the* huipil. *Lights fade in again as she finishes the completed* huipil.)

CHOMIHA: *(As she takes the* huipil *out.)* Gucumatz! Gucumatz! *(*Chomiha *places the weaving tool in the basket.)*

GUCUMATZ: Yes, Chomiha.

CHOMIHA: I finished the *huipil* for Iqui Balam. Could you tell me how I can bring it to him?

GUCUMATZ: God almighty, you are a fast learner! All right, you must go to the town of Sonsonate in El Salvador. Iqui Balam will be waiting for you before you reach the first coffee plantation.

CHOMIHA: Oh, but how can I get there?

GUCUMATZ: *(*Gucumatz *begins to offer* Chomiha *directions in the form of a very fast and rhythmic Indian "rap." During the "rap,"* Chomiha *tries to follow the complicated directions.* Gucumatz *sings.)*

Turn to the right
And then turn left
Follow the arrows
Don't miss the step!

Climb up the hill
And slide down the road
Swim the lagoon
And talk to the toad

Back to the road
And up the hill
Find a blue house

Right next to a mill

Knock three times
If you find a red door
Turn the door knob
What're you waitin' for?

CHOMIHA: *(Totally confused, returns to the same place she left at the very beginning.)* Oh, back where I started from!
GUCUMATZ: *(Playfully.)* What's wrong?
CHOMIHA: I got lost.
GUCUMATZ: Well, if you can't follow easy directions, I'll get you a map.
CHOMIHA: But, but...
GUCUMATZ: Chomiha, what's wrong?
CHOMIHA: Well, sir... I don't know how to read.
GUCUMATZ: Hmmm... *(Pause.)* Well, I have the answer. I'll call a friend who will show you the way. *(Sound of a seashell call.)* Here he is! *(A quetzal descends center stage. The bird is suspended by an invisible wire.)* A quetzal, who is our national bird, will guide you to Sonsonate.
CHOMIHA: Thank you, sir! Thank you! *(She follows the quetzal who flies around the stage in circles. She gradually begins to run in ritualistic leaps and in a few seconds stops and moves downstage.)* Quetzal, why did you stop flying? *(Pause.)* You don't want to answer, ah? Well, maybe this is Sonsonate. I don't see anybody around here. *(Pause.)* Iqui Balam! Iqui Balam! Wake up! *(Enters Iqui Balam.)*

IQUI BALAM: What do you want? Who's disturbing my siesta?

CHOMIHA: I'm Chomiha. Gucumatz sent me here. He said you would give me the Golden Coffee Bean if I wove a nice *huipil* for you. Would you like to see it?

IQUI BALAM: My, oh my... You are ambitious... All right, show me the *huipil*. (Chomiha *takes the* huipil *out of her burlap bag and places it on the downstage area.*)

CHOMIHA: Beautiful, isn't it?

IQUI BALAM: *(Imitates* Chomiha.*)* Beautiful, is not enough. I was expecting something else.

CHOMIHA: Something else?

IQUI BALAM: Perhaps a good, solid Mayan calendar.

CHOMIHA: *(To the audience.)* Perhaps a good solid alarm clock, so he doesn't sleep the day away. *(To Iqui Balam.)* Please, take this beautiful *huipil* and give me the Golden Coffee Bean.

IQUI BALAM: *(Playfully.)* Oh, you want to find the Golden Coffee Bean? All right, I'll tell you where it is. I think I left it under the lemon tree. (Chomiha *runs under an imaginary lemon tree and begins to search for the magic bean.*)

CHOMIHA: *(Disappointed.)* It's not here!

IQUI BALAM: It isn't? Well, maybe I left it under that rock. (Chomiha *moves an imaginary rock and searches for the Golden Coffee Bean.*)

CHOMIHA: It isn't there either.

IQUI BALAM: What a shame! Well, maybe you can ask some of the children in this village to help you find it.

CHOMIHA: *(To the children in the audience.)* Would you help me find the Golden Coffee Bean? *(To one of the children.)* Maybe it's hidden under your seat? *(Hopefully the children in the audience will help* Chomiha *in her search for the Golden Coffee Bean.)*

CHOMIHA: *(To* Iqui Balam *after the search is over.)* We couldn't find the Golden Coffee Bean.

IQUI BALAM: I hope I have taught you a lesson.

CHOMIHA: *(Angrily.)* Just, what I needed! Why did you make me waste my time?

IQUI BALAM: Now, my child, how dare you ask for a magic coffee bean when you don't even know how to pick plain coffee beans?

CHOMIHA: Well...

IQUI BALAM: Chomiha, I won't tell you how to get the Golden Coffee Bean unless you bring me one hundred and fifty pounds of the best coffee beans gathered in the Naranjos farms.

CHOMIHA: One hundred and fifty pounds!

IQUI BALAM: That is the minimum amount required of a coffee picker. Why should I let you get away with less?

CHOMIHA: But...

IQUI BALM: I have to continue my siesta. Wake me up when you return from Naranjos.

CHOMIHA: I don't even know how to get to Naranjos. *(Looks up and sees the Quetzal flying in circles.)* Well, here we go again! *(She begins to run using the same ritual-like leaps as in her previous journeys. After a few seconds she stops center stage and speaks to the Quetzal.)* Well, if you stopped flying, this must be Naranjos.

NARRATOR: Now Chomiha joined the coffee pickers and learned how to appreciate the value of a cup of coffee. Chomiha stands in line under the burning sun to obtain a basket and to be assigned to a section to pick the coffee beans. Although it is the end of September when the coffee plants are loaded with beans, she doesn't know the *patrón*, the boss, has assigned her a section where the bushes are almost empty.

CHOMIHA: *(To an Old Man.)* Hello, Old Man. My name is Chomiha. Could you teach me how to pick coffee beans?

OLD MAN: It's very simple my child. You just choose the ripe beans, put them in your basket and, when you fill your basket, you deposit them in a burlap bag. At four o'clock we've got to weigh the harvest of the day.

CHOMIHA: That's simple, but the branches don't seem to have that many beans left.

OLD MAN: Hmmmm... That's true. I guess you arrived too late. Other pickers have gotten the best sections. You'll have to work harder and cover more bushes than the rest.

CHOMIHA: *(Begins to pick the coffee beans.)* I can't reach the top branches...

OLD MAN: You are small... Let's make a deal. I'll gather the top branches and I'll leave the low branches for you.

CHOMIHA: That's fair. *(Chomiha, her basket under her arm, begins to pick the coffee beans. The movement becomes a dance. After the dance is over she empties the basket into a burlap bag. After a few basket loads, the lights begin to dim.)* Well, it's four o'clock. I must have the one hundred and fifty pounds by now.

OLD MAN: I'll help you put the bag on the scale. *(Chomiha, with the help of the Old Man, places the burlap bag on the scale.)*

CHOMIHA: Can you read the numbers for me please.

OLD MAN: One hundred and fifty pounds. Now you can get your money.

CHOMIHA: Oh... I don't want any money. I must bring my harvest to Iqui Balam in the town of Sonsonate.

OLD MAN: Señor Sonsonate in the town of Iqui Balam?

CHOMIHA: No, Iqui Balam in the town of... Oh, never mind...

OLD MAN: Child, you better get a small cart. It's a heavy load.

CHOMIHA: *(Finds an old cart situated upstage right.)* Do you think anyone will miss this old cart?

OLD MAN: Make sure the *patrón* doesn't see you leaving with your harvest.

CHOMIHA: I'll be careful. Thank you Old Man! Now I can get the Golden Coffee Bean.

OLD MAN: Chomiha, you are a strange child. Strange but nice. Have a good journey!

CHOMIHA: *(As she loads the cart.)* Good-bye! *(The coffee plantation* patrón *appears and discovers* Chomiha *as she tiptoes, dragging the old cart loaded with the coffee beans.)*

PATRÓN: Stop that girl! *(Runs after* Chomiha.*)* Stop! Police! Get her! Get her!

CHOMIHA: *(Running faster than the* Patrón.*)* This is what I call espresso coffee! *(To the Quetzal.)* Quetzal! Quetzal! Lead my way! (Chomiha *pulls the cart and runs in circles. After a few seconds she stops center stage.)* Well, back in Sonsonate again. I hope Iqui Balam is around. *(Calls.)* Iqui Balam! Iqui Balam! *(Enters* Iqui Balam.*)*

IQUI BALAM: Chomiha, is that you?

CHOMIHA: Yes, sir. I brought you the one hundred and fifty pounds of coffee beans.

IQUI BALAM: Hard work, wasn't it?

CHOMIHA: *¡Sí, señor!* I'll drink my coffee very slowly from now on. *(Pause.)* Now, may I have the Golden Coffee Bean?

IQUI BALAM: Sure, Chomiha. Coy will give you the Golden Coffee Bean. He is in Manto, a small town in Honduras.

CHOMIHA: *(Visibly upset.)* Honduras!

IQUI BALAM: Chomiha, where is your sense of adventure?

CHOMIHA: But...

IQUI BALAM: Follow the quetzal. Goodbye Chomiha. *(Exits).*

CHOMIHA: *(To the audience.)* Oh, I'm getting tired of running in circles and getting nowhere... I wonder if that Golden Coffee Bean is worth all of this trouble. Do you think I should continue my journey? *(Hopefully the audience will encourage* Chomiha *to continue her journey.)*

CHOMIHA: Well, I guess I haven't any other choice. *(To the Quetzal.)* Show me the way to Manto, Honduras! (Chomiha *begins to walk and then increases her walking speed until she begins to run in a ritualistic dance-like manner. After a few seconds she stops.)* Well, it was quite a trip! *(To the Quetzal.)* Are you sure this is the spot? *(Pause.)* Let's see. *(Calls.)* Coy! Coy! *(Coy enters.)*

COY: Who's there? (Chomiha *laughs in a convulsive manner.)* What do you want?

CHOMIHA: The sound of your voice makes me laugh. It reminds me of …of a monkey…

COY: I have to sound like a monkey because I am a monkey. Don't you know that's what Coy means in the language of the Quichés? So, don't mess around with me. I'm no common monkey. I'm the meanest monkey in Manto! *(Grabs a ukulele and sings a punk-rock song.)*

Hold your coconuts
Li'l chick
You'll be shaking
Like a leaf

I am coy
The meanest monkey
Who's living in the trees

I am mean
Mean, the meanest

Meanest monkey in the trees

C'mon baby
Meet King Coy
The nastiest simian
In the world

C'mon baby
Meet King Coy
The nastiest simian
In the world
Yeah! Yeah! Yeah!

(Coy jumps on top of the ukulele and breaks it.)

CHOMIHA: *(Indifferently.)* I'm very impressed... Iqui Balam sent me here. He said you would give me the Golden Coffee Bean.

COY: I've got to give you nothing! *(Pause.)* Did Iqui Balam give you anything for me?

CHOMIHA: No, he didn't.

COY: Bad news, Chomiha. I can't let you have the Golden Coffee Bean unless you do something for me. (Chomiha *has a spirited and raucous tantrum.* Coy *addresses the audience.)* What's wrong with this chick? *(To* Chomiha.*)* Don't monkey around with me! You heard what I said. Are you ready?

CHOMIHA: *(Stops her tantrum.)* I hope whatever it is, it isn't going to take a long time.

COY: The Mayan Empire was not built in one day. *(Pause.)* It's rather simple. I want you to gather a sack of the best bananas from any of the nearby plantations.

CHOMIHA: Why do you want so many bananas?

COY: You do ask a lot of questions... *(Pause.)* I'll distribute them among the homeless children of this area.

CHOMIHA: Oh, you are a nice monkey...

COY: *(Screaming.)* I'm not! I'm the meanest monkey in Manto!

CHOMIHA: All right! If I get you the bananas, may I get the Golden Coffee Bean?

COY: If you get me the bananas, we'll talk about it. Goodbye, Chomiha! I've got some monkey business to attend to. *(Exits.)*

CHOMIHA: *(To the audience.)* I thought that getting the Golden Coffee Bean was going to be easier. *(To the quetzal.)* Quetzal! Take me to the nearest banana plantation! *(Chomiha proceeds to do the same ritualistic steps that she has used previously. As Chomiha circles around the stage, lights begin to dim on her.)*

NARRATOR: Chomiha learns that she could not fill her sack because most of the bananas are used for exportation, you know, sold to other countries. *(Lights fade on Chomiha who is holding an empty burlap sack in her left hand and a banana in her right hand.)*

CHOMIHA: *(In a sad mood.)* What am I going to do? *(Pause.)* Well, let's see if I can convince Coy. *(Throws herself on the floor and melodramatically drags herself as she calls for help.)* Coy! Coy! *(Coy enters.)*

COY: What are you doing? Playing the snake?

CHOMIHA: *(Melodramatically.)* Oh, Coy! Oh, Coy!

COY: Get up at once! Why are you back so early?

CHOMIHA: Oh, Coy! Oh, Coy!

COY: Stop it! What's wrong with you?

CHOMIHA: *(Stands up and quickly recovers.)* Well, I couldn't fill my sack with bananas.

COY: Is anything wrong with the harvest?

CHOMIHA: Oh, no. There were millions of bananas. The *patrón* told me I could help load the truck and they only gave me one banana as payment.

COY: Don't feel so bad Chomiha. How do you think the rural workers feel when they have to work all year for forty dollars?

CHOMIHA: Oh, that's even worse!

COY: That's right! *(Pause.)* Well, Chomiha, the important thing is that you have tried hard.

CHOMIHA: I know, I know. But now you are not going to give me the Golden Coffee Bean. (Chomiha *throws a wild tantrum and falls on the floor with faked convulsions.)* I want the magic bean! I want the magic bean! I want the magic bean!

COY: Chill out girl! I'll forget about our agreement and I'll tell you where you can get the Golden Coffee Bean.

CHOMIHA: You don't have the Golden Coffee Bean with you?

COY: Oh, no, but for sure you can get it from Quel, the Parrot. She knows where everything is in Nicaragua.

CHOMIHA: Nicaragua! Nicaragua is so far away!

COY: Quel lives in the Village of Chinandega, near the border of Honduras, but if you have changed your mind, you can always go back home without the Golden Coffee Bean.

CHOMIHA: Oh, I wouldn't like that.

COY: So... Well, Chomiha, if you decide to visit Quel, make sure you read to her from the *Popol Vuh*, otherwise she'll refuse to give you any information.

CHOMIHA: I, I...would like to... But you see, the school was very far from our house...and...and I never learned how to read and write...

COY: Chomiha, you are going to Nicaragua, and everybody in Nicaragua is either learning to read and write or teaching the people who don't know how.

CHOMIHA: That's very nice. But I'm not a Nicaraguan.

COY: It doesn't matter. Does it?

CHOMIHA: Well, I guess not.

COY: Find yourself a teacher, learn to read and write and then go to see Quel. Bye! Bye! *(Exits.)*

CHOMIHA: Quetzal! Quetzal! Take me to Nicaragua to find a teacher. *(Chomiha circles the stage as the lights begin to dim on her. A Teacher enters stage right.)*

TEACHER: Welcome to Nicaragua! So Chomiha, you want to learn how to read and write?

CHOMIHA: Yes, I do. I know it must be very difficult and I'm afraid I'm too old and dumb to learn but...

TEACHER: Stop it! Nobody is too old to learn to read and write, and I am going to teach you.

Let's start at the beginning. Did you bring your copybook?

CHOMIHA: Yes, sir.

TEACHER: All right. Sit down, please. *(Chomiha sits on the floor.)* On the chair, please. I am going to write your name and then I want you to copy it... C H O M I H A. *(Chomiha copies her name in the copybook.)* Excellent! Now, children, have you ever taught someone to read and write? No? Well, today you are going to help me teach Chomiha the vowels of the alphabet: A, E, I, O, U. I will show you the letters, you will say the vowels and Chomiha will repeat after you. *(The audience reads the vowels.)*

CHOMIHA: A, E, I, O, U... A, E, I, O, U... A, E, I, O, U...

TEACHER: Wonderful, Chomiha! Now, you can go and read from the *Popol Vuh* to Quel.

CHOMIHA: What is the *Popol Vuh*?

TEACHER: The *Popol Vuh* is the Mayan Book of Life and the Glories of Gods and Kings.

CHOMIHA: You mean like the *Bible*?

TEACHER: Exactly, Chomiha. Like the Mayan Bible.

CHOMIHA: I must go and get Quel. But before I go I want to thank you. Now, every time I sign my name I'll think of you.

TEACHER: Good-bye, Chomiha, and good luck.

CHOMIHA: Good-bye! *(To the quetzal.)* Take me to Quel...*(Chomiha circles the stage.)* Quel! Quel! Quel must be hiding in the trees. That's what parrots usually do. Quel! Quel! *(Enters Quel.)*

QUEL: *(Reads from a big book that says: "Popol Vuh.")* Who wants me? Who wants me? Who wants me?

CHOMIHA: Oh, it's me, Chomiha. Coy sent me, and he said it's all right for you to give me the Golden Coffee Bean.

QUEL: The Coffee Bean? The Coffee Bean? The Coffee Bean?

CHOMIHA: Yes!

QUEL: No way! No way! No way! Do I owe you any favors, uhh? Uhh? Have I asked you to do anything for me? Uhh? Uhh? I don't even know you! Leave me alone! I'm reading. You don't know how to read! You must read from the *Popol Vuh*. You must read from the *Popol Vuh*.

CHOMIHA: *(To the audience.)* Children! Help me to convince Quel. Tell her to come back and talk to me. Please tell Quel: Chomiha knows how to read. Again: Chomiha knows how to read. A little louder: Chomiha knows how to read.

QUEL: *(To the audience.)* Okay, okay, I'll talk to her only because you asked me. *(Gives* Chomiha *the* Popol Vuh.*)* Well, try this.

CHOMIHA: Isn't that great I can read all by myself now. *(Reads from the* Popol Vuh.*)* "Then the mountains were separated from the water, all at once the great mountains came forth."

QUEL: Congratulations!

CHOMIHA: I'm glad you like it. Now, could you give me the Golden Coffee Bean?

QUEL: The Magic Bean? The Magic Bean? The Magic Bean?

CHOMIHA: Yes! Could I have it?

QUEL: No, no, no, Vac the Hawk has it. He lives in Costa Rica.

CHOMIHA: Costa Rica!

QUEL: That's right, right, right. Costa Rica, Rica, Rica. Bye, Chomiha. Thank you for your reading. *(Exits.)*

CHOMIHA: *(To the audience.)* Oh, brother! *(To the Quetzal.)* Quetzal! Quetzal! Why are you flying away? I guess he wants to stay in Nicaragua. Well, after all I can now find my way by reading the road signs. Off we go again. *(She begins to circle the stage, moving with the ritualized steps she has used before. She stops after a few seconds and begins to read a road sign.)* Costa Rica.

NARRATOR: Yes, we are in Costa Rica. Costa Rica is the second smallest country in Central America. *(Shows a plate to the audience.)* Do you see this colorful plate? Well, to decorate this plate, I use a complicated technique of mixing colors that my family has used for almost a century. It all started when my grandfather decided to decorate his ox cart.

CHOMIHA: Can I try?

NARRATOR: Sure. Bring the cans of paint stored in the back room. *(Chomiha exits and returns carrying a tray loaded with cans of dripping paint. She stumbles and flips the tray on the audience. Strips of colored paper come out of the cans.)*

CHOMIHA: I'm so clumsy!

NARRATOR: Don't worry. You still have some paint left.

CHOMIHA: Can I still try?

NARRATOR: Of course. *(To the audience.)* What color should Chomiha use first? *(As the audience participates,* Chomiha *will "paint" the plate with the audience's selected colors. SHE will keep the back side of the plate to the audience and will show the "finished" plate at the end.)*

NARRATOR: Oh, you are a real artist! You can take the plate with you. *(*Chomiha *dances as she shows her newly painted plate to the audience.)*

CHOMIHA: Vac must be around here. *(Calls.)* Vac! Vac! Vac! *(*Vac *appears. He wears a sinister black magician's cape.)*

VAC: Child, I am not deaf! *(Pause.)* What do you want?

CHOMIHA: I am Chomiha. Look, I brought you a present. Quel, the Parrot sent me here and she told me you could tell me where to find the Golden Coffee Bean.

VAC: Don't you go around believing everything that is said to you. Parrots talk too much.

CHOMIHA: *(Disappointed.)* You don't have the Golden Coffee Bean?...

VAC: *(Playing the villain.)* Maybe I have it... Maybe not...

CHOMIHA: What do you mean?

VAC: *(Now plays the expert magician.)* Wouldn't the Golden Coffee Bean shine if I were holding it inside my clasped fist?

CHOMIHA: Sure it would... *(There is a complete black out. Vac closes both of his hands, holding a small flashlight in each which he will turn on and off.)*

VAC: So, now you see it, now you don't! *(Lights suddenly illuminate the stage.)*

CHOMIHA: Where is it?

VAC: *(Laughing as he opens both hands to reveal they are empty.)* Gone! Never trust parrots and magic!

CHOMIHA: You never had the Golden Coffee Bean... I have painted that beautiful plate for nothing. You, like the others have taken me for a ride... I'm exhausted from walking all over Central America. What am I to do now?

VAC: *(Mimicking Chomiha.)* What am I to do now? *(To the audience.)* What should she do? Should she quit? Yes, I think so!

CHOMIHA: *(Begins to gather her belongings.)* Maybe you are right. Maybe, I should go back home.

VAC: *(To the audience ridiculing Chomiha.)* Well, isn't this a sad ending for a lovely story? This little girl is a failure, worse than a failure, she's a quitter!

CHOMIHA: *(Close to tears.)* What do you want from me? I lost all of my family in a terrible earthquake. I'm all alone!

VAC: Excuses, just excuses. You're nothing but a little kid and a quitter!

CHOMIHA: I'm not a little kid and I'm not a quitter!

VAC: Show me!

CHOMIHA: I'll show you in the same way I have shown the others that I can find my way all over Central America, all by myself! Doesn't that prove that I'm not a little kid and I'm not a quitter? And as sure as my name is Chomiha, I'm going to find the Golden Coffee Bean!

VAC: To be honest with you, Chomiha, I don't have the Golden Coffee Bean. But my friend Yak does...

CHOMIHA: Yak, Vac, Iqui Balam, Coy, Quel...

VAC: All right, all right... You may find Yak in Panama.

CHOMIHA: I hope you are not lying to me.

VAC: Why should I? Anyway, why don't you give up the whole idea of finding the Golden Coffee Bean?

CHOMIHA: Oh, no. One should never quit while there is still hope in the future. Good-bye, Vac. Enjoy your plate.

VAC: I will. Good-bye Chomiha, and good luck. *(Exit* Vac. Chomiha *proceeds to do her ritualized steps. At the end of her imaginary journey she reads from a sign post.)*

CHOMIHA: This way to the house of Yak... This way to the house of Yak. *(*Yak *enters.)*

YAK: Chomiha, welcome to Panama. I have been waiting for you.

CHOMIHA: How do you know my name?

YAK: I know everything, Chomiha.

CHOMIHA: That's nice. Probably you know where I can find the Golden Coffee Bean.

YAK: Sure, Chomiha, but first, I want you to remodel the Panama Canal.

CHOMIHA: The Panama Canal! You must be kidding!

YAK: Yes, Chomiha. I'm kidding you. In fact, I have been teasing you throughout your whole journey. *(Changes his voice and speaks like* Gucumatz.*)* Don't you recognize my voice?

CHOMIHA: But why did you do that?

GUCUMATZ: Because I wanted to teach you a lesson.

CHOMIHA: So the Golden Coffee Bean does not really exist?

GUCUMATZ: Of course, it does! And you, Chomiha, are the rich owner.

CHOMIHA: Me?

GUCUMATZ: Yes, Chomiha. You had the courage and determination to learn, work and share. Isn't that a real treasure?

CHOMIHA: Yes, now I know how to find my own unpolluted water. How to weave my own *huipil*, how to pick coffee beans, how to gather my own bananas, and how to read and write all my needs and feelings, and paint beautiful plates. Didn't I learn to work and share with all my brothers and sisters of Central America? From now on, I consider myself the richest girl in the world!

GUCUMATZ: Well said, Chomiha. That's what I call rich!

(Sings.)

To love and share will make you rich
To plow your soil
And praise your land
To gather harvest
Then sing and dance

To learn the alphabet
Holding hands
And weave and paint
The country side

To love and share
Should be your wish
To love and share
Will make your rich

To know your culture
And know your land
To know your brothers
And feel their pride

To know your history
Should be your wish
To teach your brothers
Will make your rich

GUCUMATZ and CHOMIHA: *(Sing.)*
To love and share
Should be your wish
To love and share
Will make your rich

At the end of the song, a golden coffee bush covered with thousands of gold coffee beans, descends center stage, suspended by an invisible wire.

El gato sin amigos—
The Cat Who Had
No Friends

by

Joe Rosenberg

El gato sin amigos—
The Cat Who Had No Friends*
by Joe Rosenberg

Based on a story by Teresita Gómez Vallejo
Translated and adapted for theater by
Joseph Rosenberg
Music by
John Matthew Rosenberg

Characters

ENGLISH NARRATOR
SPANISH NARRATOR
RUFO
ROTTEN TURKEY
WALRUS
ANIMALS

*In addition to the designated characters there
will be many called* Animals. *This is to say that as*

---

*"El gato sin amigos/The Cat Who Had No Friends is pub-
lished by permission of the Encore Performance Publishing.

many as there are who wish to take part in the play, all can do so at least in the roles of various animals, the particular kind to be determined by each actor and director. The English *and* Spanish Narrators *in this play complement each other dramatically by reinforcement, using a technique invented for this play. It is called interlocking narration. By this means the narrator in each language comments upon the statement made by the other by underscoring it in his/her language and adding to it.*

The play opens with a parade of Animals *down center aisle of the auditorium. The* Actors *wear large animal masks, mingle with the public, helping children wear masks, in general having fun with the public. Any kind of music may be used in this play. It can be that composed by John Matthew Rosenberg, composed especially for this play, or other music, according to the needs of the public. For the sake of selecting your own, let us say the first piece will be a conga of the variety you choose. At a designated moment the actors respond to whistles blown by the* Narrators, *return to center aisle and count off to the rhythm of the conga, in English first.*

ENGLISH NARRATOR (EN): *(After the count down reveals that Rufo is absent.)* Where's Rufo? *(None of the* Animals *know. A blowing of whistles.* Animals *count off in Spanish.)*

SPANISH NARRATOR (SN): *(After the same result.)* Dónde está el Rufo? *(Spanish Narrator's question becomes by the* Animals *a chant in English and Spanish as they form a conga line*

*and dance in a file onto the stage area. During
the dance,* Rufo *enters from the rear of the auditorium, flashes his mask right and left to the
public, swings his tail vainly, greets the public
charmingly. In a word he is your friendly, self
indulgent, lazy cat. He doesn't wear his mask
upon entering the auditorium, no, not he. Rather
he carries it by his side, jauntily revealing his
makeup, of which he is justifiably proud. On
stage, he puts the mask on, taking elaborate
bows while expertly doing his version of the
conga between the* Narrators *down stage. The
dance ends upon* Rufo's *third bow. The* Animals,
*up stage, sit, take off their masks, fan them-
selves, stretch and reinforce the following action
with comments in animal lingo.)*

EN: Hello, everybody.

SN: Hola, hola

RUFO: Meow, meow!

EN: Once upon a time...

SN: Había una vez un gato...

EN: Yes, there was a cat with a body made of rags...
(Rufo *goes limp.)*

SN: Y la cabeza al revés... (Rufo *reverses his mask.)*

EN: Backwards...his head was on backwards...

BOTH: No, no...

EN: I'm telling the story all wrong.

SN: Completamente, me equivoqué de cuento...

EN: The story we are about to tell you...

SN: El cuento que les vamos a contar es de un gato,
pero no de trapo...

EN: It's about a real, honest to goodness cat, and not just one made out of rags either. A real cat.

SN: El gato... *(Rufo bows, preens his pleasure, meows, very proud to be alive.)*

EN: Gato means cat. *(To public.)* Say it after me. Gato, cat. Come on, let me hear you...

SN: Qué quiere decir "gato"? What does gato mean?

EN: As if he doesn't know. Gato means cat. What does cat mean? Qué quiere decir cat?

SN: *(Read my lips.)* ¡Gato!

EN: Not you, them!

AUDIENCE (AUD): *(With help from* SN.*)* ¡Gato!

EN: Good ! Very good!

SP: ¿Y cómo se dice gato en inglés?

AUD: Cat!

EN: Wow! Now you have it!

SN: Bueno, si gato significa cat, pues cat significa gato. *(To* Aud.*)* ¿Verdad? Right?

EN: Right. Verdad. El gato in this story, I mean the cat...

SN: Se llama Rufo.

EN: His name is Rufo. *(Rufo bows and bows and bows, elaborately, takes off his mask to preen.* EN *steals his mask, throws it over Rufo's head to* SN *as Rufo hisses and claws. The mask goes back and forth between the* Narrators, *with the* Animals *urging them on gleefully. Finally* SN *puts the mask back on Rufo's head.)*

ALL THREE: Meow, meow.

EN: It's the same in both languages. *(Indicates audience response.)* Meow, meow!

SN: ¡Igualito!

EN: The cat in this story is called Rufo. He is very pretty...

SN: Muy bonito... (Rufo, *enchanted, lies on his back, paws up, making pleasure sounds.* Narrators *chuck him under chin and rub his belly. He becomes ecstatic.)* Y muy presumido.

EN: Let's face it. Stuck up.

SN: Muy stuck up! (Rufo *jumps up, claws ready, hisses.)*

EN: You aren't really stuck up. That's just what it says in the story, Rufo. You really aren't stuck up.

SN: No más en el cuento. De veras no es presumido. (They stroke him and he loves it.) Miren que tiene tan grandes bigotes...

EN: Look at his big moustache...and those big, green eyes!

SN: ¡Muy verdes! Los ojos como uvas...

EN: Big, big green eyes...and he's also very clean... (Rufo *preens, rolls, flexes, swaggers, purrs.)*

SN: Se lava siempre las manos antes de sentarse en la mesa... (Rufo *shows audience his paws, licks them.)* para comer su pescado...

EN: Yes, he does, he always washes his hands before going to the table to eat his fish...and this cat always eats fish...

SN: Pescado...puro pescado, nada más. Y saben por qué? Porque este gatito...

EN: This cat doesn't eat mice...

SN: ¡Nunca! ¡Nunca come ratones!

RUFO:Yuk! (*While* Rufo *displays his profound disgust* EN *pulls his tail.* Rufo *howls, runs after*

EN, *spits, claws.* SN *pulls his tail. He wheels around in pursuit. Passing* Animals *who pull his tail as he runs off stage howling.)*

SN: *(Goes down stage, indicates to public he is about to unload a state secret, at the very least.)* Bueno, pero no crean que este gato, que Rufo, este gato, es un tesoro de buenas costumbres...

EN: No indeed, don't get that idea at all! Rufo is not such a well behaved gato, you know. *(Whispers to* Public *and* Animals.) That cat, Rufo, has one very big thing wrong with him...

SN: Si, el gato Rufo tiene un defecto muy grande, grandísimo... *(Secretively.)* Voy a decirles el defecto... (Animals *gather around for the gossip, some saying "chisme, chisme.")*

EN: That cat Rufo...that cat Rufo is a...a very lazy cat. (Animals *register gratification at hearing such devastatingly humiliating gossip.)*

SN: Eso es. Un gato perezoso. Muy haragán. *(*EN *and* SN *run to center down stage.* Animals *surround them up stage.)*

EN: Give me an L! (All *pantomime the letter "L." Same for other letters.)* Give me an A! Give me a Z! Give me a Y! What's that spell? *(As* Animals *say it,* Rufo *enters, preening, yawning, takes off his mask, lies down, paws in air.)*

ALL: Lazy!

EN: What?

ALL: Lazy!

EN: *(To* Public.) I can't hear you! One more time!

ALL: *(With* Public.) Lazy!

EN: That's right! Rufo is lazy!

RUFO: *(As* Animals *repeat.)* Moi?

SN: Haragán!

EN: Haragán!

ALL: Haragán! *(Make a circle in three steps.)* Uno, dos, tres. *(Point to him. He shrugs, yawns, snores fitfully.* Animals *snore.* Narrators *imitate.)*

SN: *(Shrugs.)* Nunca tiene prisa.

EN: Never. He's never in a hurry. Every morning he gets up late. *(*Rufo *pantomimes. Dabs a little water on his face: three drops.)*

SN: Sí, se levanta tarde y lava la cara con una sola gota de agua...y, después de desyunar, se viste de domingo...

EN: As if he were going to a party, the way he gets all dressed up in his Sunday finest...

BOTH: And goes out for a walk on the avenue...se va a pasear. *(*Rufo's *actor can invent a routine. It might include* Rufo *stretching, yawning, rising, doing one stroke with a toothbrush, one spit, dampening each eye with one drop of water, cutting fish with one stroke of knife, downing fish in one gulp, cleaning mouth with one dab of napkin, preening before mirror as he puts on Sunday finest, posing in self adoration, putting mask on with loving tenderness, adjusting it this way and that way before mirror, and exiting, swinging tail jauntily.* Narrators *imitate all this. Music, perhaps jazz, something lively, like "Bugle Boy March."* Animals *wake up, each performing a simple morning task, then put on masks and exit, in single file, behind* Rocking

Robin *each punching an imaginary time clock.*
Return. Punch in. Now the stage is a work place.
Their work is to form a mobile, each doing a spe-
cific action. Rufo *enters, tries to attract atten-*
tion, but is kicked and otherwise ignored. He is
considered worthless. A toot of kazoos from the
Narrators *motivates the* Animals *to form a dif-*
ferent mobile. Rufo *tries again to horn in, but*
with similar results. Another toot and a third
mobile, with the same results. Another toot and
the Animals *collapse, as if unwound.* Narrators
wind them up. Rufo *gets in the way, wanting to*
be wound up, instead he gets a yanked tail and
runs around howling. Animals *punch out and*
exit single file behind Rotten Turkey. Rufo *tries*
to imitate, but gets his tail caught in the punch
machine, and whimpers. During the first mobile
the following dialog.)

SN: Sin importarle que en esa hora los demas estén
trabajando...

EN: That's it. He doesn't stop to consider that at
that hour all the others are working and have
no time to play with him. He's very selfish.
*(*Rufo *sniffles, feeling dejected, exits.)*

SN: Rufo sale solo. *(Both imitate his exit.)* Un día...

EN: One day, as Rufo was walking all alone by the
lake *(Enter* Rufo, *dejected, swinging his tail list-*
lessly.) he felt very lonely. (Rufo *tries various*
things to entertain himself, such as throwing a
yoyo which he does well, then trying a little more
daring stunt, then more daring until he can't
catch it and it hits him in the face, trying to

catch a bumblebee which alights on his nose and causes him to claw his nose, tearing it up, and so forth.)

SN: Se sintió muy solo, y se dio cuenta de que hacía mucho tiempo que no hablaba con nadie.

RUFO: *(Runs down right.)* Hello! *(Echo. NARRATORS shrug. He runs to down left.)* Hola! *(Same results.)*

EN: Nothing.

SN: Nada.

EN: He hadn't talked with anyone so long. And he wanted to talk with someone so badly...

SN: Sí, tenía muchas ganas de hablar con alguien, y como tenía muchas ganas, se fue a la casa de la gallina Cacareona.

EN: So he went to look for the hen, Cacareona, at her house. *(EN and SN pantomine chickens. Rufo exits left. From right enter Cacareona and Chicks to a jazz tune, perhaps "Shake It and Break It." Chicks peck around mischievously while Mama pats tortillas. Rufo enters jauntily, tries to play with Chicks, who laugh at him as he makes believe he is pulling a worm out of the ground, then they snub him.)*

EN: But in Cacareona's house he wasn't so well received at all.

SN: En casa de Cacareona no le fue muy bien. La gallina apenas lo atendió.

EN: Nobody, but nobody had any time for him. Cacareona was way behind in her schedule in the kitchen, trying to make four flour tortillas at a time.

SN: Sí, Cacareona estaba muy atareada en la cocina, preparando muchas tortillas de harina, cuatro a la vez. *(Cacareona steps on his tail as he watches, and he runs yowling out. Dance of the* Chicks *picking worms, a vigorous, funny dance. Then all but one exit.* Rufo *sneaks up on it from stage left, chases it off, stage right, then is driven back on stage by a belligerent* Cacareona. Rufo *retreats off left, disgusted that nobody wants to play with him.)*

EN: Since Rufo saw he wasn't very welcome...

SN: Como se dio cuenta que su presencia no era grata, se fue amoscado.

EN: In a huff. *(Pulls SN's shirt in back, as if to signify Rufo's tail. They imitate Rufo's angry exit, then his dejection.)*

SN: Una mañana de primavera el gato se aburría paseando solo por los jardines...

EN: He got bored walking around and around with nothing to do and nobody to play with, all by himself... *(Enter* Rufo, *stalking an imaginary bird, pouncing upon it, then chasing his tail, then deciding he was deluding himself, scratches at a flea, then yawns, sits, shrugs, meows, licks his paws. Enter* la Mariposa Amarilla, *the butterfly. He watches her with fascination as she dances.)*

EN: And so he tried to play with the butterfly...

SN: Amarilla...pero... *(Dance of the* Butterfly. *Could be to the tune of "Glowworm" or some such.* Rufo *chases after* Butterfly, *but every time she stops to preen and he tries to catch up with her to say hello, or ask her if she wants to play monopoly or checkers,* Amarilla *takes off for another place, with the result that he falls on his face. At the end of the dance there is a desperate chase.* Amarilla *exits, and* Rufo *follows. There is an off stage crash sound,and then* Rufo, *somewhat dazed, staggers on stage, panting for breath. During the dance, the following dialog occurs.)*

SN: Todo fue inútil...

EN: Totally useless...

SN: La Mariposa estaba trabajando, y se fue revoloteando de flor en flor...

EN: Here, there, here, there, there, here, she had no time for him, none at all, no way, José. It was useless totally, totally useless.

Upon his return on stage, Rufo *shrugs, lies down at down center. Enter a* Mouse *to a lively tune, something on the order of "The Lonely Bull" if he is a tough guy, "Sugar Plum Fairy" if it is a Minnie Mouse type.* Mouse, *seeing* Rufo, *runs out fearfully, comes back cautiously, then musters up the courage to touch* Rufo, *runs out, runs back, tiptoes to* Rufo, *touches moustache, observes that* Rufo *does not seem concerned, decides to play with moustache, pulls at it, gets no response, pinches* Rufo's *nose, gets no response, shrugs, yanks* Rufo's *tail, no response, asks audience if he/she should make a taco or a hot dog of the tail, then asks for ingredients, the more outlandish the better, such as a peanut butter taco or a hot dog with syrup, then asks public if he/she should bite, pumps the public for response three or four times, each time becoming a little braver, then bites. Still no response.* Rufo *merely picks up his tail, swings it forward and sighs.* Mouse *shrugs, says something to the effect that there's no fun around here today, then exits, grandstanding all the way, as if he/she has just become the latest national hero.*

SN: Rufo ni apetito tenía, de lo triste que estaba.
EN: He was one totally stressed out cat.
SN: Pero totally. *(Rufo sits up. Narrators try to console him, stroking him. He does not respond.)*
EN: One afternoon...
SN: Sí, una tarde...
EN: One afternoon, when the sun decided to come out and then hide behind the clouds...

Enter Sun, *then* Clouds, *to a slow tune, perhaps a fox trot. Sun can be bossy or sweet, maybe even a valley girl.* Clouds *dance around* Sun *who weaves out and then is surrounded, and this pattern is repeated with variations. In the skirmish between* Sun *and* Clouds *to determine whether it will be a sunny or a cloudy day,* Sun *can say things like* "Watch out, I'll burn ya!" *or sweet things if she is that type.*

SN: Cuando el sol se ponía entre las nubes, al gato se le ocurrió...
EN: To visit the walrus. When the sun was behind the clouds Rufo decided to visit the walrus...

Rufo *runs off stage with energy. The* Walrus *enters, perhaps to a lumbering jazzy tune like "Two Jim Blues." * Walrus *is slow, lumbers in, perhaps* *with a cane and spats and a bowler hat to dance a chorus step or two with the* Narrators, *perhaps some other kind of walrus, like a mechanic who wears a baseball cap backwards. Lots of possibilities. Whatever he looks like, he likes to roar a good deal. He steps down from stage to play with the kids, giving his mask to them and encouraging them to roar with him.*

EN: Walrus... (Children *repeat.)*

SN: Oso marinero... (Children *repeat.)*

EN: And now...

SN: Ahora... *(Enter* Rufo, *rowing an imaginary sail boat, and using his tail as if it were an imaginary fog horn.)*

EN: Here he comes...

SN: Mira, no más, ahí viene Rufo remando...

EN: Rowing all over the place, looking for the walrus...

SN: Buscando al oso marinero...

EN: And when he got where he could see the walrus...

SN: *(Pantomimes use of fog horn.)* Cuando vio al oso marinero, lo llamó desde unas rocas...

EN: Called out to the walrus from the rocks...

RUFO: ¡Hola, oso marinero! Hey there, Mr. Walrus! *(Walrus* roars. Rufo *tries to roar, but it comes out meow.)*

RUFO: You want to play, Mr. Oso Marinero, Mr. Walrus, sir? I have a fish for you, pescadito, fishy, fishy, fishy! I'll give you Jaws if you play with me.

EN: But did the walrus want to play with Rufo?

SN: ¿Qué creen? ¿Creen que el oso marinero quería jugar con el gato, Rufo? Definitiva y rotundamente... *(Walrus shakes his head in negation and invites kids to join him. They roar. Sun and Clouds shake heads and roar. Sun can say things like "No way, José.")*

SN: ¿Y por qué no?

EN: You know why not.

SN: Dime, dime, dime, dime...

EN: Porque, when the walrus saw him he roared...

SN: Rugió, rugió...

EN: Guess what!

SN: ¡Adivinen! Listen! ¡Escuchen!

EN: Listen, listen, ¡escuchen!

WALRUS: This is no time to play, this is a time to work!

EN: Work.

SN: Work.

WALRUS: ¡Trabajar!

ALL: *(Except* Rufo.) ¡Trabajar! Work! ¡Trabajar! ¡Trabajar!

Walrus: Váyase, éste no es tiempo para jugar, sino para trabajar! *(Narrators signal kids to repeat the word "trabajar," then "work." Rufo starts to row off, bawling.)*

RUFO: Nobody wants to play with me! *(Rows off.)*

EN: And so the cat sailed away in a hurry!

SN: ¡A toda vela!

RUFO: *(Returns.)* Oops! *(Sails out, bawling.)*

SN: El gato se fue a toda vela en su barquito.

Narrators *pantomime* Rufo *sailing away and bawling, playing at it with the kids.* Clouds, Sun *and* Walrus *play with* Children. *Then* Walrus *dances with* Narrators *during which time* Sun *and* Clouds *exit. Then* Walrus *goes roaring off stage, comes in for another bow, and more applause.* Narrators *imitate him. Enter* Rufo, *dragging his tail, tries to console himself by wearing shades, which, when he looks in the mirror, scare him. He takes center stage, despondent.* Narrators *cross right of* Rufo, *mock cry on each other's shoulders.*

SN and EN: He was dying of sadness...

SN: Sí, se moría de tristeza al sentirse tan apartado de los demas.

EN: Because he felt as if he didn't have a single friend in this whole world.

SN: Ni un solo amigo tenía, ni uno.

RUFO: *(Bawls, stamping his feet like an angry child.)* ¡Ay, qué solo estoy! Nobody wants to talk to me even... I don't even have one single friend. ¡No, ni un solo amigo tengo! *(Bawls and bawls, stopping occasionally to clear his nose.)*

EN: That's how he was crying when...when...guess what? That's how he was crying when...

SN: Así lloraba el gato cuando el Rotten Turkey... (Can be called Nervous Vulture or somesuch.)

EN: The Rotten Turkey appeared!

Enter Rotten Turkey *in very modern dress, dancing to a tune similar to the song, "Rockin Robin" or somesuch. Dances with* Narrators, *then down into the auditorium with* Public. Narrators *continue dancing on stage. After a while* Rotten *dances back on stage, pecks at* Rufo's *tail. During the following* Rotten *will speak in one language, any one, and one of the* Narrators *will speak in the other.* Rotten *leads the public in response.*

RUFO: Waaaah! Waaahhhhh! I don't have any friends, ni un solo amigo! Ay de mí. Ay de mí! I'm so lonely!

ROTTEN TURKEY (RT): *(Continues to dance.)* Claro que sí...

EN: Of course you don't.

RT: Eso te pasa por pereza...porque eres muy haragán.

EN: Because you're lazy...

RT: ¡Y desconsiderado!

EN: And you don't care what other people think or feel, only yourself.

SN: Eso, es muy egoísta.

RT: Muy egoísta. *(*Animals *support this.)* ¿Te parece razonable?

EN: Does it seem right to you?

SN: ¿Te parece razonable?

RT: Que los demás estan trabajando y tú sin hacer nada?

EN: That everybody works...

SN: And you don't do anything at all.

EN: Lazy bum?

SN: ¿Haragán? *(*Rufo *bawls and kicks his feet in a cat tantrum.)*

RT: ¿No te das cuenta de que molestas a los demás en las horas de trabajo?

EN: Doesn't it matter to you, doesn't it matter to you, huh, huh, huh?

SN: That you bother everybody during their work? And you go to sleep...

EN: When they want to work?

RT: ¿Te parece bien?

ALL: Huh, huh, huh? (Rufo *goes into an extravagant tantrum.*)

RT: Si trabajaras y fueras un gato útil a los demás... (Rufo *stops suddenly, looks at him, at the others, then bawls harder.*)

ALL: Un gato útil... (Rufo *bawls harder and harder.*)

RT: Tendrás muchos amigos. (Rufo *stops bawling, looks.*)

PUBLIC and ANIMALS: *(At cue from Rotten Turkey.)* ¡Muchos amigos! ¡Muchos amigos. ¡Tendrás muchos amigos! (Rufo *points to himself.*) ¡Muchos, muchos, muchos! (Rufo *bawls in disbelief.* Rotten Turkey, Animals, Public *shrug, not knowing what to do with* Rufo.)

EN: Let's give it to this lazy cat, Rufo, so he stops being so lazy.

RT: ¡Le jalamos la cola!

SN: La cola, la cola! (Rufo *runs off before anyone can touch him. He screeches all the way. All laugh and clap.*) Pues, ya se animó! *(Laughter.)*

EN: That's what it takes to make him pay attention! As if we really were out to get him! Now that we woke him up, I wonder if he'll stop being lazy.

SN: ¿Tu, qué crees? *(Addresses* Public.)

EN: Let's dance some more with the Rotten Turkey while we're waiting to find out. *(Music.* Narrators *do a solo dance with* Rotten Turkey. *Then* Rotten *dances off, waving good-bye.)*

ALL: Bye, Rotten Turkey, bye! ¡Adiós! ¡Adiós! Hasta la bye bye!

SN: ¡Adiós, Rotten Turkey!

Narrators *continue to dance.* Rufo *peeks out, does a meow, gets no response, then a few more, more audibly, no response, licks his paws, then with determination, joins the* Narrators *in the dance of the Rotten Turkey. The dance over,* Rufo *waves to the* Narrators, *then to the* Public *with a wink as he goes off.*

RUFO: Bye, bye, bye. *(Exits and returns, knocks his knees a couple of times, then looks at* Public *through an imaginary telescope made of his tail, waves.)* Adiós, hasta luego, adiosito. *(Exits.)*

SN: Creo que Rufo ya ha comprendido...

EN: Me too, I think Rufo got the message that he had been living without considering other people...

SN: Que había vivido equivocado, y decidió terminar con un defecto grande como es el ser haragán.

EN: And he decided to stop being a lazy cat. *(Asks* Public.*)* What do you think?

SN: ¿Piensan ustedes que es posible?

EN: Listen...

SN: ¡Ay, escuchen!

Jazz tune of Animals *entering to work. Something on the order of "Salutation March." Enter* Animals *in a single file behind* Rotten Turkey. *They form in a circle and start to do a mobile.* Rufo *enters and takes a position in the center of the circle, leading them in their changes.*

EN: And from that day on...

SN: Desde ese mismo día el gato empezó a trabajar.

EN: He did. He began to work, and now he is one of the best workers. (Narrators *toot.* Animals *perform different job.)*

EN: And now the cat in this story is a very happy cat...

SN: Muy contento y feliz, feliz, el gato de este cuento...

EN: He works and leads an organized life, in which there is time for work when others work, and time for play.

SN: Es un gato trabajador con una vida organizada, y tiene mucho amigos.

EN: Muchos, muchos. He has lots and lots of friends. (Animals *play at leap frog with him.)*

EN: And they get together after work, and on Sundays and holidays.

SN: Se reúnen mucho para jugar. El día de su último cumpleaños.

EN: When he had his birthday, everybody came to play with Rufo and they brought him a big birthday cake. (Rotten Turkey, *who had left during leap frog, enters with cake and lighted candles.)*

SN: ¡Qué grandote el pastel que le trajeron!

EN and SN: And they all sang together, cantaron, cantaron...

ALL: (Public *included.)*

Happy birthday to you,
Feliz cumpleaños a ti,
Happy birthday, dear Rufo,
Feliz cumpleaños a ti.

RT: Come, let's watch Rufo blow out the candles! *(Rufo huffs and puffs and blows them out, perhaps with help.* All *cheer.* Rufo *bows to public and blows a kiss.)*

ALL: Hurrah for Rufo!¡ Arriba, arriba Rufo! *(Conga music.* Animals *all form in conga line, headed by Rufo. They wave to* Public *on their way out.)*

EN: And that's how our story ends.

SN: *(Putting Rufo's head on himself/herself.)* Con eso termina este cuento.

155

Song of the Oak—
El canto del roble
by
Roy Conboy

Song of the Oak—El canto del roble
by Roy Conboy

Characters

GUSTAVO [GUS] (a boy who doesn't like raking leaves)

SHE-WHO-REMEMBERS (a storyteller)

CHORUS #1 & #2 (two actors)

LEAVES #1 & #2 (singing and dancing oak leaves)

TÍO SOL Y TÍO VIENTO (Uncle Sun and Uncle Wind)

SEÑORA Y SEÑOR VÍBORA (two snakes who live under the oak tree)

PEPE Y PITA ARDILLA (two squirrels who like acorns)

SEÑORITA OSA (a bear who just woke up)

ROJO Y AZUL (two birds)

Casting

This play is designed to be performed by 4 actors.

1. Gustavo
2. She-Who-Remembers/Senorita Osa
3. Chorus #1/Leaf #1/Tío Viento/Señora Víbora/ Pita/Rojo
4. Chorus #2/Leaf #2/Tío Sol/Señor Víbora/ Pepe/Azul

Songs

1. "El Canto del Roble/The Song of the Oak"
2. "The Detective Song"
3. "Do the Snake!"
4. "Acorn Song"
5. "Just Like a Human!"
6. "Arriba en el Cielo!/Up In the Sky!"

Scene One

The scene is an oak tree.

She-Who-Remembers *(Ella-Quien-Recuerda) enters playing a drum. She is accompanied by two actors who act as a* Chorus. *Lines will be spoken in rhythm with the drums.*

SHE:
  Once upon a time,
  Not long ago,
  There was a very very beautiful oak!
CHORUS 1: Pues, una vez...
CHORUS 2: No hace mucho tiempo...
CHORUS 1: Había un roble muy bonito!
SHE: With beautiful leaves...
CHORUS 2: Con hojas bonitas...

SHE: In a beautiful field…
CHORUS 1: En un campo bonito…
SHE: By a beautiful river.
CHORUS 2: Al lado de un río bonito.
ALL: Yeah!

Gus *enters and sits under the oak.*

SHE:
Once upon a time…
Not long ago…
There was a grumpy boy named Gustavo.
CHORUS 1: Pues, una vez…
CHORUS 2: Había un muchacho…
CHORUS 1: Gruñón se llama Gustavo.
SHE: Sitting by that tree…
CHORUS 2: Sentado por el roble…
SHE: In that beautiful field…
CHORUS 1: En el campo bonito…
SHE: By that beautiful river.
CHORUS 2: Al lado del río bonito.
ALL: Yeah!

Drums stop.

GUS: Yeah, that's right. I'm Gustavo. So what?
SHE: Así es. Now this Gus person wasn't very happy…
GUS: No, no estoy muy contento.
SHE: Because he didn't like anything.
GUS: Es verdad. No me gusta nada.
CHORUS 1: Gus, do you want to play some baseball?

GUS: ¿Quiero jugar béisbol? No. No me gusta béisbol.

CHORUS 2: Gustavo, do you want to play some music with me?

GUS: ¿Quiero tocar música? ¿Contigo? Olvídalo. No me gusta la música.

CHORUS 1: Gus, ¿quieres bailar?

GUS: Do I want to dance? No way! I don't like dancing.

SHE: Gustavo, esto es un bonito roble, ¿no?

GUS: A beautiful oak tree? No. I don't like this oak tree.

SHE: ¿No te gusta? ¿Por qué?

GUS: Why? Porque todas las mañanas...

SHE: Because every morning...

Gus *gets out a rake.*

GUS: Tengo que rastrear las hojas de ese roble bonito.

SHE: He has to rake up all the leaves from that beautiful tree.

Chorus *become the leaves.*

LEAF 1: ¿Hojas?

LEAF 2: Leaves?

LEAF 1: Somos nosotros.

LEAF 2: That's us.

SHE: Now that job sounds pretty easy, hunh?

GUS: ¿Fácil?

SHE: But it wasn't.

GUS: ¡No es fácil!

SHE: Because every morning when the sun is warm...

GUS: Porque en la mañana cuando el sol está caliente...

LEAVES: Mmmmm, el sol...

SHE: And the wind is soft...

GUS: Y el viento está blandito...

LEAVES: Mmmmm, el viento...

SHE: Then the leaves begin to dance and sing.

GUS: Las hojas comienzan a bailar y cantar.

SHE: "El Canto del Roble"

GUS: "The Song of the Oak"

Music. The Leaves *begin to dance and sing.* Gus *chases them with his rake.*

Song #1: "The Song of the Oak"

LEAVES:
In the morning
When the wind blows,
¡Canta tu canto!

GUS: Hey!

LEAVES:
In the morning
When the leaves shake,
¡Baila tu baile!

GUS: Wait!

LEAVES:
Woo woo, lo llamamos
El Canto del Roble.

GUS: No!

LEAVES:
Cha cha cha, we call it

The Song of the Oak Tree.

GUS: Stop!

LEAVES:
En la mañana,
Viento loco,
Sing your crazy song!

GUS: Hey!

LEAVES:
En la mañana,
Hojas lindas,
Dance your crazy dance!

GUS: Stop!

Interlude.

GUS: Oh sí, creen ustedes que esto es chistoso, ¿no?

SHE: I suppose you think this is funny, don't you?

GUS: ¡Pero, yo no!

SHE: But he doesn't!

GUS: Cómo puedo rastrearlas...

SHE: How can he rake them up?

GUS: ¿Cuando ellas están cantando ese canto?

SHE: When they're singing that song?

GUS: ¿Y bailando ese baile?

SHE: And dancing that dance?

GUS: ¿Cómo?

SHE: How?

GUS: How?

SHE: ¿Cómo?

Song #1: "The Song of the Oak" (continued)

LEAVES:
In the morning

163

When the wind blows,
¡Canta tu canto!
GUS: Hey!
LEAVES:
In the morning
When the leaves shake,
¡Baila tu baile!
GUS: Wait!
LEAVES:
Woo woo, lo llamamos
El Canto del Roble.
GUS: No!
LEAVES:
Cha cha cha, we call it
The Song of the Oak Tree.
GUS: Stop!
LEAVES:
En la mañana,
Viento loco,
Sing your crazy song!
GUS: Hey!
LEAVES:
En la mañana,
Hojas lindas,
Dance your crazy dance!
GUS: Wait!
LEAVES:
Woo woo, lo llamamos
El Canto del Roble.
Cha cha cha, we call it
The Song of the Oak Tree.
GUS: No!

LEAVES:

> Woo woo, lo llamamos
> El Canto del Roble.
> Cha cha cha, we call it
> The Song of the Oak Tree.

GUS: Stop!

LEAVES:

> Cha cha cha, we call it
> The Song...
> Of the Oak Tree!

GUS: Stop!!

Song #1 ends.

LEAF 1: Well, Gustavo? ¿Te gusta nuestro canto?

LEAF 2: Do you like our song?

GUS: No, no, no, no, no! I don't like it!

The Leaves *are highly insulted.*

LEAF 1: Well!

LEAF 2: Pues!

LEAF 1: How rude!

LEAF 2: ¡Qué brusco!

LEAF 1: If you don't like our song...

LEAF 2: Si no te gusta nuestro canto...

LEAF 1: Fine!

LEAF 2: Bueno!

LEAF 1: We'll go!

LEAF 2: ¡Iremos!

GUS: You will? All right!

LEAVES: ¡Sí! Adiós!

The Leaves *exit.*

GUS: Hey, can you believe it? They're gone. Las hojas se fueron. Fresh. Now I can sit back and take it easy. Yeah!

Gus *sits back and takes it easy.*

Scene Two

She-Who-Remembers *begins to play her drum again.*

SHE:
Yes, once upon a time,
Not long ago,
All of the leaves went away...

Pues, una vez,
No hace mucho tiempo,
Todas las hojas se fueron...

And then I remember...
Y entonces recuerdo...
The world got very very cold...
El mundo se puso muy muy frío.

Drums end. She-Who-Remembers *shivers dramatically.*

SHE: Oooo woah! Oooo wow! Oooo yow!

Gus *sits up.*

GUS: Wow! ¡Que frío!
SHE: ¡Qué freezing!
GUS: ¡Qué freezing!
SHE: ¡Qué frío!
BOTH: ¡Ayyyyy!

GUS: Hey, who are you?

SHE: ¿Quién soy yo? Me llamo Ella-Quien-Recuerda.

GUS: You're called She-Who-Remembers? Why are you called that?

SHE: ¿Por qué? Porque es mi trabajo recordar.

GUS: Because it's your job to remember things?

SHE: That's right. Y lo recuerdo todo.

GUS: And you remember everything?

SHE: Simón.

GUS: Wow. You must be pretty smart.

SHE: ¿Inteligente? ¿Yo? Pues, es verdad.

GUS: Then, can you tell me why it's so cold now?

SHE: Puedo decirte porque hay tanto frío ahorita? No.

GUS: No?

SHE: No. Pero tal vez si se lo preguntas a tu Tío Sol y a tu Tío Viento…

GUS: If I ask my Uncle Sun and my Uncle Wind? But where will I find them?

SHE: Where?

She beats her drum. Tío Sol *and* Tío Viento *enter.*

SOL: Hola, Gustavo. Soy Tío Sol.

VIENTO: Hello, Gus. Soy Tío Viento.

SOL/VIENTO: Sigh…

GUS: Wow! How did you do that?

SHE: Tu pregunta, Gus. Tu pregunta.

GUS: Oh yeah. Tíos, ¿saben ustedes por qué hay tanto frío ahorita?

SOL: Do we know why it's so cold? Oh sure.

VIENTO: It's because we're both so sad.

SOL: Es por que los dos estamos tan tristes.

SOL/VIENTO: Sigh...

GUS: But I don't understand. No entiendo. Están tristes, y por eso...

SOL: And so I don't feel like shining.

GUS: ¿Tú no quieres brillar?

VIENTO: And I don't feel like blowing.

GUS: ¿Y tú no quieres soplar?

SOL/VIENTO: That's right. Sigh...

GUS: Pero, ¿por qué están tan tristes?

SOL: Why are we so sad?

SOL/VIENTO: Because the leaves are gone!

GUS: ¿Porque las hojas se fueron?

SOL: Ay, me gustaba verlas bailar.

GUS: You liked to watch them dance?

VIENTO: Ay, me gustaba oírlas cantar.

GUS: And you liked to listen to them sing?

SOL/VIENTO: "El Canto del Roble."

GUS: "The Song of the Oak?"

SOL: Sí. Pero ahora se fueron...

VIENTO: But now they're gone...

SOL: Y por eso estamos muy tristes...

VIENTO: And so we are very sad...

SOL/VIENTO: Sigh...

GUS: But that's silly.

SOL: ¿Necio? Well!

VIENTO: Pues!

SOL: How rude!

VIENTO: ¿Qué brusco!

SOL: Just like a human!

VIENTO: ¡Claro!

SOL/VIENTO: ¡Adiós, Gustavo!

She-Who-Remembers *beats her drum.* Tío Sol *and* Tío Viento *exit.*

GUS: But wait!

SHE: ¡Esperen!

GUS: You can't leave yet!

SHE: ¡Todavía no pueden irse!

GUS: You have to warm things up!

SHE: ¡Necesitan calentar el mundo otra vez!

GUS: Ay, they're gone.

SHE: Ay, se fueron. What are you going to do?

GUS: ¿Qué puedo hacer? Pues, no sé.

SHE: You don't know?

GUS: No. But I think someone has to find the leaves and bring them back.

SHE: ¡Qué buena idea! Alguien tiene que hallar las hojas y traerlas.

GUS: That's right. Pero, ¿quién puede hacerlo?

SHE: Who can do it? You!

GUS: Me?

SHE: Sí!

She-Who-Remembers *beats her drum.*

SHE: ¡Gustavo!

GUS: What?

SHE:

Ahora te nombro a ti...

Today I appoint you...

¡El Detective Doble Zero Dos!

GUS: Detective 002?

SHE:

¡Y te mando que halles las hojas!
And I order you to find the leaves!
Y que devuelvas "El Canto Del Roble"!
GUS: And bring back "The Song of the Oak?"

Drums end.

SHE: ¡Sí! ¡Buena suerte, Detective Doble Zero Dos!
GUS: Gracias, ¡pero cómo comienzo?
SHE: How do you start?
GUS: ¿Y dónde las hallo?
SHE: And how do you find them?
GUS: ¿Y qué hago?
SHE: And what do you do? Pues...

Music.

Song #2: "The Detective Song"

SHE:

When you want to know the answer.
When you want to know the way.
When you're feeling all confused,
And you don't know what to say...

What do you do?
You ask a question!
Mr. Detective,
You ask a question!

¿Qué haces?
¡Una pregunta!
El Detective,
¡Una pregunta!

170

BOTH:

    Cuando quieres el camino.

    Cuando quieres la respuesta.

    Cuando te sientes muy revuelto,

    Y no sabes qué decir...

    ¿Qué haces?

    ¡Una pregunta!

    El Detective,

    ¡Una pregunta!

    What do you do?

    You ask a question!

    Mr. Detective,

    You ask a question!

    Mr. Detective,

    You ask a question!

Song #2 ends.

GUS: All right! Questions. I have to ask questions.

Scene Three

She-Who-Remembers *plays her drum again.*

SHE:

    Y entonces recuerdo...

    And then I remember...

    La investigación comenzó...

Drum stops. She hands a magnifying glass to Gus.

GUS: Okay! It's time to start the investigation. And my first question...

SHE: Tu primera pregunta...

GUS: ¿Dónde están los rastros?

SHE: Where are the clues?

GUS: ¡Ajá! ¡Aquí en el suelo!

SHE: Here on the ground?

GUS: The last known location of the leaves.

SHE: Ah, el último lugar de las hojas. Muy inteligente, ¿no?

He searchs. She sits down to watch.

GUS: Ah ha! A clue! It looks like a trail. Parece que es una trocha. But these are very long feet. Pies muy largos. Hmmmm.

He follows the trail.

Señor *and* Señora Víbora (Mr. and Mrs. Snake) *slither in from under the tree. They do not yet see* Gus, *and he does not yet see them.*

VÍBORAS: Tsssss!

SRA. VÍBORA: What's going on?

SR. VÍBORA: ¿Qué pasa aquí?

VÍBORAS: Tsssss!

SRA. VÍBORA: Why is it so cold?

SR. VÍBORA: ¿Por que hace tanto frío?

SRA. VÍBORA: Do you know?

SR. VÍBORA: ¿Sabes tú?

SRA. VÍBORA: Or you?

SR. VÍBORA: ¿O tú?

VÍBORAS: Tsssss!

GUS: Hmmmmm.

Las Víboras *see* Gus *and slither over to him.*

SRA. VÍBORA: Well...

SR. VÍBORA: Pues...

SRA. VÍBORA: What have we here?

SR. VÍBORA: ¿Qué tenemos aquí?

VÍBORAS: Yuck, it's a human! Tsssss!

GUS: Aaaarrgh! ¡Víboras! Snakes!

VÍBORAS: Tsssss!

GUS: Help! Help! Get them off me! Get them off.

SRA. VÍBORA: Hey, ¿qué pasa?

SR. VÍBORA: ¿Tienes miedo?

GUS: Yes, I'm afraid. Snakes give me the creeps.

SR. VÍBORA: Los "creeps"? That's not very nice.

SRA. VÍBORA: We only want to know...

SR. VÍBORA: No más queremos saber...

SRA. VÍBORA: Where is the song?

GUS: ¿Dónde está el canto?

SR. VÍBORA: And what happened to the leaves?

GUS: ¿Qué pasó con las hojas?

SRA. VÍBORA: And why is it so cold?

GUS: ¿Por qué hace tanto frío?

VÍBORAS: ¡Sí!

GUS: Pues...

VÍBORAS: Yes?

GUS: Well...

VÍBORAS: Yes?

GUS: ¡Un momento! ¡Un momento! Yo soy el Detective Doble Zero Dos!

SR. VÍBORA: You're Detective 002?

GUS: ¡Claro! ¡Y yo hago las preguntas aquí!

SRA. VÍBORA: And you'll ask the questions here?

GUS: ¡Sí!

SRA. VÍBORA: Okay, okay. Whatever you say.

SR. VÍBORA: Con calma. Con calma.

GUS: Bueno. Now, who are you?

SR. VÍBORA: ¿Quiénes somos? Somos Señor y Señora Víbora.

SRA. VÍBORA: We're Mr. and Mrs. Snake.

GUS: And what are you doing here?

SR. VÍBORA: ¿Que hacemos aquí?

SRA. VÍBORA: We live here.

SR. VÍBORA: Sí, sí. Vivimos aquí.

GUS: Here?

SRA. VÍBORA: That's right. We have a nice little hole right under this oak tree.

GUS: Tienen un hoyito simpático debajo de este roble?

SRA. VÍBORA: Yes. And we would invite you in, but you're a human, and you wouldn't fit.

GUS: That's okay. I don't want to crawl into any smelly old hole.

SR. VÍBORA: ¡¿Hoyito apestoso?!

SRA. VÍBORA: Well!

SR. VÍBORA: ¡Pues!

SRA. VÍBORA: How rude!

SR. VÍBORA: ¡Qué brusco!

SRA. VÍBORA: Just like a human!

SR. VÍBORA: ¡Claro!

GUS: Hey, hey, I'm sorry.

SRA. VÍBORA: Listen to me, you little delinquent. This happens to be an excellent neighborhood.

SR. VÍBORA: Éste es un vecindario muy muy excelente.

GUS: Yes, yes. Estoy seguro.

SRA. VÍBORA: And this is a beautiful oak tree...

SR. VÍBORA: Éste es un roble bonito...

SRA. VÍBORA: Cool during the summer…

SR. VÍBORA: Fresco en el verano…

SRA. VÍBORA: And warm during the winter…

SR. VÍBORA: Y cálido en el invierno…

SRA. VÍBORA: Which is very important to snakes.

SR. VÍBORA: Que es muy importante para las víboras.

GUS: It is? But why?

SRA. VÍBORA: Why? Because we have cold blood.

GUS: ¿Sangre fría?

VÍBORAS: ¡Híjole!

Music.

Song #3: "Do the Snake!"

SRA. VÍBORA: Sangre fría…

SR. VÍBORA: Cold blood…

VÍBORAS:
>That's why we stay
>Out of the sun.

SRA. VÍBORA: Sangre fría…

SR. VÍBORA: Cold blood…

VÍBORAS:
>If we don't want to boil
>We have to run.

>Hey, do The Snake, yeah!
>La Víbora! Sssss…
>Hey, do The Snake, yeah!
>La Víbora! Sssss…

SRA. VÍBORA: Cold blood…

SR. VÍBORA/GUS: Sangre fría…

175

VÍBORAS/GUS:
>No nos gusta
>Un día caliente.

SRA. VÍBORA: Cold blood...

SR. VÍBORA/GUS: Sangre fría...

VÍBORAS/GUS:
>Nos sentimos como
>Dos tortillas.
>
>Hey, do The Snake, yeah!
>La Víbora! Sssss...
>Hey, do The Snake, yeah!
>La Víbora! Sssss...
>
>Hey, do The Snake, yeah!
>La Víbora! Sssss...
>Hey, do The Snake, yeah!
>La Víbora! Sssss...

Song #3 ends.

GUS: Yeah, I get it. If you have cold blood like Señor y Señora Víbora...

SR. VÍBORA: Si ustedes tienen sangre fría...

GUS: You don't like weather that's too hot or too cold.

SR. VÍBORA: No nos gusta el tiempo muy caliente ni muy frío.

GUS: And so...

SR. VÍBORA: Y por eso...

SRA. VÍBORA: Good-bye, Gustavo.

SR. VÍBORA: Adiós, Gustavo.

GUS: But wait! ¡Espera! You can't go yet. I need some clues.

SR. VÍBORA: ¿Necesitas algunos clues?

GUS: Sí. ¿Pueden ayudarme?

VÍBORAS: Puessssss...

SRA. VÍBORA: This is all we have.

SR. VÍBORA: Esto es todo lo que tenemos. *(They give him a bag.)*

GUS: Oh. Thank you. But what is it?

SRA. VÍBORA: It's a hole.

SR. VÍBORA: Es un hoyo.

GUS: A hole? Well. Muchas gracias. Es un clue importante. Pero, ¿qué puedo apprender de este hoyo?

SRA. VÍBORA: What can you learn from this hole? You're the detective.

SR. VÍBORA: Tú eres el detective.

SRA. VÍBORA: It's your job to figure it out.

SR. VÍBORA: Es tu trabaja resolver eso.

GUS: Yeah, but...

SRA. VÍBORA: Just remember! "El hoyo es la casa".

GUS: "The hole is the home?"

SRA. VÍBORA: That's right.

VÍBORAS: Buena suerte. Adiós.

GUS: Thank you. Adiós. *(Las Víboras exit.)*

Scene Four

She-Who-Remembers *plays her drum.*

SHE:
Once upon a time...
Not long ago...
Detective Gus had a clue...

Pues, una vez...
No hace mucho tiempo...
El detective tenía una clue...

Drums stop.

GUS: "The hole is the home?"
SHE: "El hoyo es la casa"?
GUS: What kind of a clue is that?
SHE: ¿Qué tipo de clue es esa?
GUS: Híjole...

Two Squirrels (Pepe y Pita Ardilla) *enter carrying lots of suitcases.*

She-Who-Remembers *sits down to watch.*

PEPE: Come on, come on, come on!
PITA: Okay, okay, okay!
PEPE: ¡Más rápido! ¡Más rápido!
PITA: ¡Con calma! ¡Con calma!

They drop some suitcases and stop to pick them up.

PEPE: ¡Ay, por Dios!
PITA: Holy cow!

They drop more suitcases.

PEPE: ¡Cuidado! ¡Cuidado!
PITA: You be careful! It was your fault!
PEPE: ¿Mi culpa? No way!
PITA: Oh yeah?

They square off to fight.

GUS: Hey, excuse me? Excuse me?

PEPE: Ay, ¿qué quieres, hombre?
PITA: What do you want?
GUS: I am Detective Double-O Dos.
PEPE: ¿Detective Doble Zero Dos?
GUS: That's right. Y necesito su ayuda.
PITA: You need our help?
GUS: That's right.
PEPE/PITA: Olvídalo.
GUS: Forget it?
PEPE/PITA: Buenos días.

Pepe *and* Pita *square off to fight again.*

PEPE: Come on, come on, come on!
PITA: Okay, okay, okay!
GUS: ¡Señores!
PEPE/PITA: ¿Sí?
GUS: Perdónenme, ¿pero qué tenían en sus valijas?
PEPE: What do we have in our suitcases?
PITA: Pues, Señor Detective...

They stop fighting and open a suitcase. It is full of acorns.

PEPE/PITA: Voilá!
GUS: ¡Híjole! ¿Qué son éstas?
PEPE: Éstas son las mejores bellotas del mundo.
GUS: The finest acorns in the world?
PITA: Simón.
PEPE: For sure.
PITA: ¿Quieres comprar una docena?
PEPE: Do you want to buy a dozen?
GUS: Oh, no thank you...
PITA: ¿O dos docenas? ¿Tres docenas?

GUS: No gracias…

PEPE: ¡Es un estupendo precio!

PITA: It's a wonderful price!

PEPE: ¡Es una fabulosa ganga!

PITA: It's a fabulous deal!

GUS: No, thank you! Just tell me, where are you taking them?

PEPE: ¿Dónde las estamos llevando? Ay, no sabemos.

PITA: No, we don't know, Señor Detective.

PEPE: Pero no podemos quedarnos aquí.

PITA: But we can't stay here.

PEPE: Porque hace mucho frío.

PITA: Because it's very very cold.

PEPE: Y las hojas se fueron.

PITA: And the leaves are gone.

GUS: Pues, entiendo. yo también estoy buscando esas hojas.

PITA: You're looking for the leaves?

GUS: Yes. So Tío Sol and Tío Viento can warm the world up again.

PEPE: ¡Ay, qué bueno!

PITA: Tal vez quieres comprar una bellota sabrosa para Tío Sol y Tío Viento.

PEPE: Maybe you'd like to buy a tasty acorn for them.

GUS: Yuck!

PEPE/PITA: Yuck?

GUS: They don't want any acorns. No quieren bellotas. Acorns are nasty.

PEPE/PITA: ¿Feas?

PEPE: Well!

PITA: ¡Pues!

PEPE: How rude!

PITA: ¡Qué brusco!

PEPE: Just like a human!

PITA: ¡Claro!

GUS: Now wait a minute...

PEPE: For your information...

PITA: Para tu edificación...

Music.

Song #4: "The Acorn Song"

ARDILLAS:

They don't look important.

They aren't very famous.

And nobody sends them a birthday card.

No parecen importantes.

No tienen fama.

Y nadie recuerde sus nombres.

But acorns, acorns, acorns...

They'll grow up to be

Some great oak trees...

Bellotas, bellotas, bellotas...

Un día serán

Robles...

ARDILLAS/GUS:

They're only a seed.

Not a car or a ring.

Not even a refried bean.

181

No más son semillas.
No carros o anillos.
Ni siquiera frijoles.

But acorns, acorns, acorns…
They'll grow up to be
Some great oak trees…
Bellotas, bellotas, bellotas…
Un día serán
Robles…
Un día serán
Robles…

Song #4 ends.

GUS: Wow, I never realized that acorns turn into oak trees.
PEPE: ¡Claro que sí, Gustavo!
GUS: You know what? I'll bet an acorn would make a very important clue.
PITA: Ah, sin duda, Señor Detective.
PEPE: Here, Gus. One fabulous acorn, no charge.
GUS: Ay, muchas gracias.
PITA: De nada. Just remember!
PEPE: ¡Recuerda! "La bellota es la semilla".
GUS: "The acorn is the seed?"
PEPE/PITA: ¡Claro que sí! Hasta luego!
GUS: ¡Adiós!

Pepe *and* Pita *exit.*

Scene Five

She-Who-Remembers *plays her drum.*

SHE:
>And then I remember...
>Y entonces recuerdo...
>Más preguntas y más preguntas y más preguntas...

Drums end.

GUS: ¿El hoyo es la casa?
SHE: The hole is the home?
GUS: ¿La bellota es la semilla?
SHE: The acorn is the seed?
GUS: Hmmmm...
SHE: Hmmmm...
GUS: I need more clues.

Gus *looks for more clues.* She-Who-Remembers *tosses some footprints on the ground.*

SHE: Sí, necesitas más clues. Como ésto, y ésto, y ésto...

Then she puts on a mask and becomes Señorita Osa (Ms. Bear).

Gus *finds a footprint.*

GUS: ¡Ay ay ay! ¿Qué es ésto? Una huella. A footprint.

He finds another footprint.

GUS: ¡Híjole! Another footprint! Es muy grande, ¿no?

He finds another footprint.

GUS: ¡Ay chihuahua! ¡Otra huella! Hmmm, ¿qué piensan? ¿Qué tipo de animal es? ¿Amistoso? Friendly? ¿Contento? Happy?

Señorita Osa (Ms. Bear) *roars.*

OSA: Roar!
GUS: Or maybe not so friendly.
OSA: Roar!
GUS: And not so happy.

Señorita Osa *grabs* Gus.

OSA: You!
GUS: Me?
OSA: ¿Quién eres tú?
GUS: Who am I? Yo soy Gustavo.

She shakes Gus.

OSA: Mucho gusto, Gustavo.
GUS: Mu-mu-mu-mu-mucho gusto. ¿Y quién eres tú?
OSA: Who am I? Yo soy Señorita Osa.
GUS: Ms. Bear? How nice to meet you.

She shakes him again.

OSA: Thank you.
GUS: De-de-de-de-de nada.
OSA: Now tell me, Señor Gustavo, where is the song?
GUS: ¿Dónde está el canto?
OSA: And where are the leaves?
GUS: ¿Dónde están las hojas? Pues, ¡no sé!
OSA: You don't know? Aaaarrgh! I'll bite your arm!

GUS: No! No me muerdas el brazo!

OSA: No? Aaaarrgh! Then I'll bite your leg!

GUS: No! No me muerdas la pierna!

OSA: No? Aaaarrgh! Then I'll bite your head!

GUS: No! No me muerdas la cabeza!

OSA: No? Then where can I bite you?

GUS: ¿Dónde puedes morderme? ¿Por qué necesitas morderme?

OSA: Why do I have to bite you? Because I'm grumpy!

GUS: Tú eres gruñón, ¿sí?.

OSA: And I'm furious!

GUS: Tú estás furiosa, ¿sí? Pero ¿por qué?

OSA: ¿Por qué? Porque dormí todo el invierno...

GUS: Because you slept all winter...

OSA: Y soñé todo el invierno...

GUS: And you dreamed all winter...

OSA: De ese bonito y fabuloso y fantástico...

GUS: About that beautiful and fabulous and fantastic...

OSA: "Canto del Roble"!

GUS: "Song of the Oak?"

OSA: Pero ya que estoy despierta...

GUS: But now that you're awake...

OSA: No oigo el canto.

GUS: You don't hear the song.

She shakes Gus *again.*

OSA: ¡¡¡Y por eso no estoy contenta!!!

GUS: You-you-you-you-you're not happy?

OSA: No!

GUS: Pero, Señorita Osa, ¿qué de especial tiene ese
    canto?
OSA: What is so special about that song? Well!
GUS: Pues?
OSA: How rude!
GUS: ¿Qué brusco?
OSA: Just like a human! ¡Claro!

Music.

Song #5: "Just Like a Human!"

OSA: Just like a human, yeah!
GUS: Como humano, ¿sí?
OSA: Just like a human, yeah!
GUS: Como humano, ¿sí?
OSA:
    You never think
    About the trees!
    You never think
    About the leaves!
    You never think…
    You never think
    About
    All the other living things!
GUS: Just like a human, yeah!
OSA: Como humano, ¡sí!
GUS: Just like a human, yeah!
OSA: Como humano, ¡sí!
GUS:
    ¡No pensamos nunca
    De las osas!
    ¡No pensamos nunca
    De las hojas!

¡No pensamos nunca...
De todos
Los otros
Que viven con nosotros!
OSA: Just like a human, yeah
GUS: Como humano, ¡sí!
OSA: Just like a human, yeah!
GUS: Como humano, ¡sí!
OSA/GUS:
   Just like a human!
   ¡Como un humano!
   Just like a human, yeah!

Song #5 ends.

GUS: Wow. You know you're right. Before this I never thought about what the leaves or the bears or the trees or the squirrels might want. But from now on I will.
OSA: Muy bien, Gustavo.

   Señorita Osa *shakes* Gus *again.*

OSA: Pero, ¿dónde esta el canto?
GUS: ¡No-no-no-no-no entiendes, Señorita Osa! Yo soy el Detective Doble Zero Dos!
OSA: ¿Detective Doble-O Dos?
GUS: Sí. ¡Y estoy buscando las hojas!
OSA: And you're looking for the leaves? Ahhh!
GUS: Pero necesito clues.
OSA: Ohhhh, you need clues! Pues, aquí.

   She gives him a handful of dirt.

GUS: ¿Qué es ésto?

OSA: That's dirt.
GUS: ¿Tierra?
OSA: Sí. Es un clue muy estupendo, ¿no?
GUS: Yes, yes. You're right. Dirt is a wonderful clue.
OSA: Claro que sí. ¡Y recuerda! "La tierra es la comida".
GUS: "The dirt is the food?"
OSA: ¡Así es! So long.
GUS: Adiós.

She shakes him one more time.

OSA: ¡Busca las hojas!
GUS: ¡Sí-sí-sí-sí-sí! I'll find the leaves!

She lets him go.

GUS: I-I-I-I-I-I promise!

Señorita Osa *takes off her mask and becomes* She-Who-Remembers *again.*

Scene Six

GUS: Okay, now we're going to see if I can figure this out...

Rojo *and* Azul, Two Birds, *enter circling.*

ROJO: Rrraaa! ¡Qué frío!
AZUL: Aaarrr! ¡Qué freezing!
GUS: Vamos a ver si puedo aprender...
ROJO: Mis alas están casi congeladas!
AZUL: My wings are almost frozen!

GUS: I have three important clues. Tengo tres clues importantes…

ROJO: Ay mira, Azul.

AZUL: Hey look, Rojo.

GUS: The dirt is the food.

ROJO: La tierra es la comida.

GUS: The hole is the home.

AZUL: El hoyo es la casa.

GUS: The acorn is the seed.

ROJO/AZUL: La bellota es la semilla.

GUS: ¡Híjole!

ROJO: Rrraaa! ¿No entiendes, Gus?

AZUL: Aaarrr! Don't you understand, Gustavo?

GUS: No, no entiendo. Hey, ¿quiénes son ustedes?

ROJO: Hola, me llamo Rojo.

AZUL: Hi, my name is Azul.

GUS: Mucho gusto. Yo soy Gustavo.

ROJO: Yes, we know. You're looking for the leaves, right?

AZUL: Estás buscando las hojas, ¿si?

GUS: That's right. But I can't find them.

ROJO: ¿No? Pero tienes todos los clues.

AZUL: But you have all the clues.

GUS: I know. But that's not enough.

ROJO: ¿No es bastante?

GUS: No! I need more!

AZUL: ¿Necesitas más?

GUS: Yes!

ROJO: Well!

AZUL: ¡Pues!

ROJO: How rude!

AZUL: ¡Qué brusco!

GUS: I know, I know. Just like a human!

ROJO/AZUL: ¡Claro!

GUS: Hey, I'm sorry. But I just don't understand. No puedo entender.

ROJO: ¡Rrraaa! ¡Ven con nosotros, Gustavo!

AZUL: ¡Aaarrr! Come with us, Gus!

They grab Gustavo.

GUS: Wait! Where are we going?

ROJO: A dónde vamos? ¡Al cielo!

GUS: Up into the sky?

AZUL: ¡Simón!

GUS: But, but, but…

ROJO: ¡Rrraaa! Let's go!

AZUL: ¡Aaarrr! ¡Vámonos!

GUS: But my mother didn't give me permission to fly!

ROJO/AZUL: ¡Arriba!

All three *take off.*

GUS: Woooooaaaahhhh!

Music. They sing as they fly.

Song #6: "¡Arriba en el cielo!/Up in the Sky!"

ROJO/AZUL:
There's so much to see
When you open your eyes—
So many living colors,
The world is a prize.

GUS:
Hay tanto para ver
Cuando abro mis ojos—

Colores vibrantes,
El mundo precioso.

ALL:

Arriba, arriba, arriba
En el cielo.
Up, up, up
In the sky.
Arriba, arriba, arriba
En el cielo.
Fly, fly, flying
So high.

ROJO/AZUL:

Look at the oak trees
Growing everywhere.
Every time they breathe
They're making the air.

GUS:

Mira los robles
En todas partes.
¡Cuando respiran
Hacen el aire!

ALL:

Arriba, arriba, arriba
En el cielo.
Up, up, up
In the sky.
Arriba, arriba, arriba
En el cielo.
Fly, fly, flying
So high.
Fly, fly, flying
So high.

Fly, fly, flying
So high.

Song #6 ends.

Rojo, Azul *and* Gus *land.*

GUS: All right! Thank you! That was great.
ROJO: De nada.
AZUL: You're welcome.
GUS: And now I understand!
ROJO/AZUL: ¿Ahora entiendes?
GUS: Yes! Trees give us air and homes and beauty...
ROJO: Los robles nos dan aire y casas y belleza...
GUS: Because we need those things.
AZUL: Porque necesitamos esas cosas.
GUS: And if I want the leaves to come back...
ROJO: Y si quieres que las hojas vuelvan...
GUS: I have to plant a new oak tree!
AZUL: ¡Tienes que plantar un roble nuevo!
GUS: Am I right?
ROJO/AZUL: Muy bien, Gustavo!
SHE: Muy bien, Gus!

Rojo *and* Azul *exit.*

She-Who-Remembers *plays her drum. She and* Gus *begin to chant. And as they chant he plants the new tree.*

GUS: And then I remember...
SHE: Y entonces recuerdo...
GUS: The dirt is the food...
SHE: La tierra es la comida...
GUS: The hole is the home...

SHE: El hoyo es la casa...
GUS: The acorn is the seed!
SHE: ¡La bellota es la semilla!
GUS: That's how we make...
SHE: Es como hacemos...
GUS: A new oak tree!
SHE: ¡Un roble nuevo!
GUS: And now every spring...
SHE: En las primaveras...
GUS: The leaves will return...
SHE: Las hojas volverán...
GUS: And sing "The Song of the Oak!"
SHE: ¡Y cantarán "El Canto Del Roble"!

Music.

GUS: Listen!
SHE: ¡Escucha!

The Leaves *enter. All sing and dance.*

Song #1: "The Song of the Oak" (Reprise)

LEAVES:
> In the morning
> When the wind blows,
> ¡Canta tu canto!
>
> In the morning
> When the leaves shake,
> ¡Baila tu baile!

ALL:
> Woo woo, lo llamamos
> El Canto del Roble.

Cha cha cha, we call it
The Song of the Oak Tree.

En la mañana,
Viento loco,
Sing your crazy song!

En la manana,
Hojas lindas,
Dance your crazy dance!

Interlude.

SHE: Yes, the leaves returned...
GUS: Las hojas volvieron...
SHE: And sang the song...
GUS: Y cantaron el canto...
SHE: And Uncle Sun and Uncle Wind were happy...
GUS: Y Tío Sol y Tío Viento estaban contentos...
SHE: And the world was warm again...
GUS: Y hacía calor en el mundo otra vez...
SHE: And all because of Gustavo...
GUS: ¡El Detective Doble Zero Dos!
SHE: ¡Viva!

Song #1: "The Song of the Oak" (Continued)

ALL:
  In the morning
  When the wind blows,
  ¡Canta tu canto!

  In the morning
  When the leaves shake,
  ¡Baila tu baile!

Woo woo, lo llamamos
El Canto del Roble.
Cha cha cha, we call it
The Song of the Oak Tree.

En la mañana,
Viento loco,
Sing your crazy song!

En la mañana,
Hojas lindas,
Dance your crazy dance!

Woo woo, lo llamamos
El Canto del Roble.
Cha cha cha, we call it
The Song of the Oak Tree.

Woo woo, lo llamamos
El Canto del Roble.
Cha cha cha, we call it
The Song of the Oak Tree.

Cha cha cha, we call it
The Song...
Of the Oak Tree!

Song #2 (Reprise) ends.

ALL: Adiós, amigos!

Curtain.

Fred Menchacha y Filemón

de

Jose G. Gaytán

Fred Menchacha y Filemón
de José G.Gaytán

¡Hola, Amigos!

Tengo mucho gusto de estar aquí con ustedes, pero no podré quedarme mucho tiempo. Dejé a mis pollos y mis marranos solos en el rancho. Si no regreso pronto a darles de comer se pueden salir del corral y comerse el maíz y los frijoles que planté en el campo. Son muy malos los animales. Me pueden dejar hasta sin casa ni petate.

También dejé a mi burro, mi Filemón, allá en la pasada. Quería traerlo aquí pa' que lo conocieran, pero allá el de la migra me dijo que necesitaba sus chots.

—¿Y pa' qué son esas shots, señor?—le pregunté.

—Puede estar malo.

—Pos, ¿malo de qué? A mi burro no se le suben ni la pulgas.

—No le hace—me dijo el hombre. Así es que tuve que dejarlo allá, amarrado en un poste. Ojalá y no se lo roben.

¡Ah! Ni me presenté. Qué falta de educación. Pueden llamarme Fred Menchaca. Mi nombre completo es Federico Antonio José Panchito González Menchaca Smith, pero mis amigos me dicen Fred Menchaca.

¿Sabían que pa' cruzar la frontera de México a los Estados Unidos necesitan pasaporte? Sí. El Americano en la frontera me dijo—Give me your papers, ¡Dame tus papeles!

Y yo, creyendo que quería el periódico que traía doblado dentro del cinto, se lo di.

—¡No, el periódico no! ¡Tus papeles, el pasaporte!

—Ah, pos no traigo pasaporte, señor.

—Pos entonces no puedes pasar pa' los Estados Unidos.

—Pero tengo que pasar, mi oficial. Los estudiantes en (nombre de institución) me están esperando.

—Bueno, entonces te voy a dar un permiso provisional, pero tienes que regresar de inmediato y entregarme el permiso, do otro modo te meto en la cárcel.

Mi Filemón y yo hemos ido a muchos lugares. Una vez nos subimos en un barco grandote y cruzamos el mar. Allá del otro lado hay un país que se llama Francia. ¿Han oído hablar de ese país? Allá la gente habla francés y les gusta abrazar y dar un beso en la mejilla cuando saludan.

Al bajarnos de ese barcote, la gente vino hacia Filemón y mi y dijeron—Bonjour, Fred Menchaca. Bonjour, Filemón.

Y me dieron un abrazo y un besote en la mejilla. De primero no estaba yo muy, cómo se dice, cómodo, pero antes de darme cuenta, ya estaba abrazando y besando a la gente. Los abrazos son buenos. Son buenos para la salud. A menos que abraces a la gente que no le gusta que la abracen. Como a mi tío Pánfilo. Es muy malo. Siempre pone la mano sobre su pistola, listo para balacear al que lo ofenda. Cuando llegué a México y le dije buenos días a mi tío Pánfilo con un abrazo y un beso en el cachete, me empujó y me dijo—si me vuelves a abrazar; te doy un moquete!

Así es que no siempre es saludable abrazar a la gente. Pero cuando te abrazan ellos también, se siente re-padre.

¡Ah! En Francia me querían tanto que hasta me escribieron una canción. ¿La han oído? Lleva mi nombre. Se canta así:

Fred Menchaca, Fred Menchaca
Dormez vous? Dormez vous?
Sonnez les matines, sonnez les matines
Ding, Dang, Dong. Ding, Dang, Dong.

Bueno. Tengo que ir a ver a mi burro. Lo dejé solo demasiado tiempo. Espero que no haya pateado a nadie. Patea muy duro. Una vez íbamos él y yo al pueblo a una fiesta. Iba yo sobre su lomo. Me dormí un poco y lo guié directamente hacia un nopal. Se llenó la nariz de espinas y empezó a brincar lleno de coraje. Al brincar me caí y me pegué en la cabeza. Luego, cuando me estaba levantando,

Filemón me pateó en mi . . . ¿cómo se llama? . . . aquí.

Desde entonces no me duermo cuando viajo en burro.

La caravana

de

Alvan Colón

La caravana
de Alvan Colón

This play for children was initially based on the poem "La Elegía del Saltimbanqui," by the Puerto Rican poet Luis Palés Matos.

The version that follows was written by Alvan Colón Lespier in Spanish with songs and some dialogue in English.

During performances for school children, we developed a version totally in English, one in Spanish and one bilingual.

The play can be performed with a minimum of three actors and two musicians.

The basic costume for all performers is the traditional Vejigante costume and masks of the Feasts of Santiago of the coastal regions of the island of Puerto Rico. When interpreting other characters, the actors don particular elements that define that character, i.e., top-hat, cape, hats, ribbons and a bright umbrella.

The music is based on typical coastal rhythms, plena *and* bomba, *and the instruments are:* pan-deros *(hand held drums), congas, accordion and drum set, (trap set is sufficient).*

The set consists of a bare stage and a six-foot folding ladder which is painted in bright colors.

Personajes

CARAVANA
SALTIMBANQUI
BEATRIZ
VEJIGANTE
MARTÍN
ACTRIZ
ACTOR

CARAVANA:

Por senderos y montes sin parar
en busca de le gran ciudad
sabremos que es la gran ciudad
sabremos que es la gran ciudad
al ver la gente y luz brillar.

SALTIMBANQUI: Yo, man, chill out, con calma, yo tengo el control.

BEATRIZ: Creo que deberíamos buscar…

SALTIMBANQUI: Yo sé el camino. Tú, ¡sígueme!

BEATRIZ: Por favor, déjame ver el mapa. Mira, pa'llá. Ahora sí que estamos perdidos. ¿Qué vamos a hacer ahora?

SALTIMBANQUI: No tengas miedo. Y soy el único, el gran Mr. Saltimbanqui. Yo te guiaré. Allá veo las luces. ¡¡¡A la carga!!!

Toco, toco, etc.

SALTIMBANQUI: Yo man... No me vengas a con coco. Además, yo no como sardinas. Pero, si me ayudas tendrás una buena recompensa...

VEJIGANTE: Muy bien, me decían ustedes que necesitaban ayuda.

SALTIMBANQUI: Mi nombre es Mr. Saltimbanqui y ésta es mi ayudante Beatriz. Comenzamos nuestra jornada hace muchos días por senderos y montes sin parar en busca de la gran ciudad. Cuando de pronto nos cogió la gran tormenta.

VEJIGANTE: ¿No tienen un mapa?

SALTIMBANQUI: Claro que tenemos un mapa, pero está viejo. A Beatriz se le olvidó cambiarlo.

BEATRIZ: Ja, él no sabe la diferencia entre un mapa viejo y un mapa nuevo. Lo que pasa es que él no sabe leer.

VEJIGANTE: ...Pero antes...

SALTIMBANQUI: Yo te voy a pagar cuando lleguemos a la ciudad. Allí hay mucho dinero.

BEATRIZ: Pero tú tienes dinero. Yo lo vi.

SALTIMBANQUI: No le hagas caso. Todavía está un poquito mareada por la tormenta.

VEJIGANTE: Yo no necesito dinero. Les mostraré el camino y me hacen un cuento.

SALTIMBANQUI: ¿Qué sé yo de cuentos? ¿Tú sabes alguno? (Beatriz..*Telita, etc.*) Muy bien, lo que tienen que hacer es seguir el camino hasta la orilla del río, allí se encontrarán con Martín Pescador. Díganle que yo los envié y pregúntenle si los puede llevar a la otra orilla del río en su bote. (*Mientras* Saltimbanqui *y* Beatriz *caminan hacia la orilla del río,* Vejigante *se coloca la capa y el gorro de* Martín Pescador. *Toma la escalera y la coloca de lado en el piso, entra y se sienta y se hace como si estuviera pescando.)*

VEJIGANTE: Are you Martín Pescador? Yo soy Mr. Saltimbanqui. Ésta es mi ayudante Beatriz. Vejigante nos envió. Él dice que usted nos puede ayudar a cruzar el río que nos lleva a la gran ciudad de Onglishtown. BEATRIZ. LLEGAMOS. MIRA LA GENTE, MIRA EL SOL, MIRA LA CALVA DE AQUEL SEÑOR. ATENCIÓN, ATENCIÓN…NIÑOS Y NIÑAS, ATENCIÓN.

BEATRIZ: Estimado público. Éste es el gran Mr. Saltimbanqui que viaja de pueblo en pueblo con sus famosos trucos mágicos.

SALTIMBANQUI:
Soy Mr. Saltimbanqui,
El mago de la Caravana.
Sorpresas traigo por doquier,
proezas mágicas de ayer.
Les presento a Beatriz,
caravanera muy feliz,
y si me permiten pues
con magia los deleitaré.

Y ahora voy a necesitar toda su cooperación. Hey, you!

MARTÍN: ¿Quién, yo?

SALTIMBANQUI: Pues claro, tú. Sujeta ésto con ambas manos. Y con mi látigo invisible lo partiré en dos. Muy bien, 25 centavos por favor.

MARTÍN: ¿Que yo tengo que pagarte a ti?

SALTIMBANQUI: Claro que sí, ¿qué tú te crees, yo hice todo esto de gratis?

MARTÍN: Un momentito. Tú hiciste la mitad y yo hice la otra y no hubieras podido hacerlo sin mí porque yo fui quien te traje a este pueblo. Por lo tanto, tú eres quien me debe pagar a mí.

SALTIMBANQUI: Pero tú estás loco. Yo soy el gran Mr. Saltimbanqui, el único. Esto es solo el principio. Ahora Beatriz, mi ayundante caminará la cuerda floja. *(Juntos ellos tienden un pedazo de cuerda imaginaria, la levantan en el aire y luego la bajan al suelo y, mientras dé un tamborileo, Beatriz se balancea en ella y pasa de un lado al otro.)*

BEATRIZ: Estimado público, ahora el gran Mr Saltimbanqui desafiará la muerte. Saltará desde la escalera y caerá de cabeza en este vaso de agua. *(Tamborileo, Saltimbanqui sube la escalera, concentra y salta, pies adelante hacia la copa. Beatriz intenta a convencer al público a aplaudir. Notando la reacción, Saltimbanqui castañetea y, con una palmada fuerte, hypnotiza a Beatriz.)* Estimado público, los poderes del Saltimbanqui no tienen límite. Presten atención, pues ahora el gran Mr. Saltimbanqui los llevará al mundo mágico de...

SALTIMBANQUI: ¡La telepatía, so boba!

BEATRIZ: ¡La telepatía, so boba!

SALTIMBANQUI: Tú eres la boba, no ellos.

BEATRIZ: Tengo hambre, tengo sed, estoy cansada, quiero dormir.

SALTIMBANQUI: *(Snap.)* Yo tengo palabra de honor y siempre cumplo lo prometido. Pero por unos centavos más les mostraré algo nunca antes visto. Mi asistente Beatriz me vendará los ojos y yo voy a leer su mente. *(Trucos.)*

BEATRIZ: Muy bien, Mr. Saltimbanqui, concéntrese, por favor. Estoy señalando a... *(Un niño.)* Continuemos, Mr. Saltimbanqui, concéntrese y diga al público presente qué color es éste... ¡VERDE! Y ahora el más difícil acto telepático. Concéntrese, Mr. Saltimbanqui, e identifique la forma que estoy describiendo... ¡CÍRCULO!

BEATRIZ: Tengo sed. Estoy cansada. Tengo hambre. No aguanto más. No aguanto más. *(*Saltimbanqui *empujaba a* Beatriz *hacia su límite sin saber lo que podría pasar.)*

SALTIMBANQUI: Estimado público, ahora Beatriz los deleitará con... *(*Beatriz *se desmaya.)* Pero Beatriz, y ¿qué es lo tuyo? Estamos en el medio del show. Vamos, arriba, a trabajar. No puedes hacerme esto. Ah, ¿sí? Pues, si no te levantas, se acabó. Estás despedida. *(Musica.)* Hey, you, ¿quieres trabajo?

VEJIGANTE: Yo ya tengo trabajo. Yo canto las historias de mi pueblo.

SALTIMBANQUI: ¿Y tú le llamas a eso trabajo? Nadie le hace caso a tus historias. Además, no son importantes. ¿A quién le importa el pasado?

VEJIGANTE: ¿Verdad a ustedes? *(Al* Público.*)* ¿A ustedes les importa el pasado? ¿Les importan las historias de su pueblo?

SALTIMBANQUI:
Historia a mí
Yo se quién yo soy
y soy como soy.

¿Con libros a mí?
¿para qué leer?

Ponerse a aprender,
Eso está demás.
¿Por qué has de pensar
si me tienes a mí?

BEATRIZ: No entiendes nada. No quiero perder el tiempo. Quiero aprender historia y ciencia. Eso es muy importante.

SALTIMBANQUI: Yo, man. Importante es lo que uno come, lo que uno siente. Eso es lo importante. Mira, yo sé muchas cosas y las tengo aquí. Si te quedas conmigo, no tendrás que aprender nada. Yo pienso por ti.

BEATRIZ: Si no pienso, jamás aprenderé y jamás creceré.

SALTIMBANQUI: Pero si ya tú creciste.

BEATRIZ: Yo quiero crecer por dentro.

SALTIMBANQUI: Si creces por dentro, reventarás como un globo.

BEATRIZ: Bueno, me voy. Págame lo que me debes.

SALTIMBANQUI: ¿Estás segura que te quieres ir? Vas a estar sola.

BEATRIZ: Yo no estaré sola. Y si necesito ayuda, ahí está Vejigante.

SALTIMBANQUI: Bueno, después no digas que no te lo advertí. *(Música.)*

BEATRIZ:
Esto no puede ser,
yo merezco algo mejor.
todo el pueblo estuvo aquí
para ver esta función.

Las ganancias yo las vi,
tú las tienes por ahí.

SALTIMBANQUI: Cálmate, chica.

BEATRIZ: Pero tú prometiste pagarme por mi trabajo.

SALTIMBANQUI: Pero si ya te pagué.

BEATRIZ: Pero aquí lo que hay es cuarenta y siete centavos. ¿Y el resto?

SALTIMBANQUI: Pues lo usé, para comprar mi... nuestra comida, el vestuario.

BEATRIZ: Este vestuario está requeteviejo.

SALTIMBANQUI: ¿Cómo te atreves a contradecirme? Malagradecida. No eras nadie antes de conocerme. Todo lo que sabes me lo debes a mí. Yo te enseñé el mundo. Yo te di comida. I provided you with a place to sleep. When you are with me that's all the money you will need. Just imagine how I feel. Put yourself in my position...

BEATRIZ: ¿Qué?

SALTIMBANQUI: Ponte en mi lugar. (Vejigante *brinca de la escalera y hace congelar a* Saltimbanqui.)

BEATRIZ: Pues, yo me voy a poner en tu sitio a ver cómo es que uno se siente...

SALTIMBANQUI: Hold it... No me gusta este juego. No, basta... Hey, yo', what the... (*Música.*)

BEATRIZ:
Oh, flaco Saltimbanqui
del circo de la aldea,
se acabó tu alegría,
terminó tu cabriola.
Ya no asustas a nadie,

has perdido la gracia.
Los niños en la calle
ya dominan tu magia.

VEJIGANTE: Y como decimos en Puerto Rico...se viró la tortilla. *(Ahora es* Beatriz *que manda.)*

SALTIMBANQUI: Atención...estimado público...presento la gran, la única Beatriz.

BEATRIZ: Gracias, gracias. Y ahora mi asistente Saltimbanqui ejecutará el salto mortal...y caerá dentro de este vaso de agua.

SALTIMBANQUI: Tengo hambre, tengo sed...estoy cansado. Quiero dormir.

BEATRIZ: Vamos, arriba. A trabajar. No puedes hacerme ésto.

VEJIGANTE: Pero, ¿qué es lo que haces?...

BEATRIZ: Cuando yo estaba cansada, él me mandó a hacer cosas y trabajar...entonces ahora voy a... *(*Vejigante *para la acción. Improvisa con el* Público *y hace preguntas sobre el cambio. Por ejemplo, "¿Así es la mejor manera de crear el cambio? ¿Hay otras maneras, otras soluciones al problema?")*

ACTRIZ: Hmmm. Que si Beatriz cambió las cosas... Si se fija, cuando ella le quitó el poder a Saltimbanqui, empezó a hacerle lo mismito que él le hacía a ella.

ACTOR: O sea, que en realidad las cosas no cambiaron. Lo que hicieron fue que cambiaron de lugar.

ACTRIZ: Y cambiar de lugar no es lo mismo que cambiar las cosas. Digo, si ustedes le van a hacer a otros lo mismo que le hacen a ustedes.

VEJIGANTE:

Toco, toco, toco, toco
Vejigante come coco

(Actores toman las posiciones que tuvieron antes de quedarse congelados, y cuando el Vejigante da el señal, siguen con la obra.)

BEATRIZ: Yo creo que la caravana puede ser de los dos...

SALTIMBANQUI: ¿De los dos? ¡Jamás! Yo soy el Mister Saltimbanqui, el único.

BEATRIZ: Ambos hacemos el trabajo, así que debemos compartir el dinero y la fama.

SALTIMBANQUI: ¡Jamás! No me voy a rendir.

BEATRIZ: No tienes nada que rendir. Porque yo lo tomé todo. Yo tengo el control. Pero quiero que trabajemos juntos. Como iguales.

SALTIMBANQUI: ¿Como iguales? Yo necesito una ayudante.

BEATRIZ: Yo te ayudo a tí y tú me ayudas a mí.

SALTIMBANQUI: I don't know...

BEATRIZ: Y si se te ocurre hacer lo que hacías antes... se acabó... para siempre... ¿De acuerdo?

SALTIMBANQUI: De acuerdo.

TODOS: *(Cantan)*

Toco, toco, toco, toco
Vejigante come coco.

Vamos muchachos pa'la marina
A comer pan y sardinas.

.

El día que se robaron

los colores

de

Héctor Santiago

Para Emily por un mundo mejor

El día que se robaron los colores
de Héctor Santiago

Personajes

ACTOR
RENÉ (niño terrícola)
CANELO (su perro)
TINGO TILINGO (feroz pirata)
TILINGO TINGO (desalmado cowboy)
LOCUTOR DEL NOTICIERO
VENDEDORAS 1, 2 (desesperadas viejecitas)
ESTUDIANTE
POLICÍA DE TRÁNSITO
PINTOR
MARCIANOS 1, 2, 3 (con zancos)
KLAPKLIP (niña marciana)
TRESTRES (animal de Urano)
URANOS (con sombrillas)
DIONOS (caballo con alas)
PLUTONIANOS (con espejuelos)

Esta obra está concebida para un gran espectáculo visual, como un juego que explotará los posibilidades del teatro infantil: títeres, esperpentos, marionetas, sombras chinescas, luz negra, cine, etc. Se desea lograr la participación de los espectadores. Cada descripción visual en el diálogo puede estar acompañada de su efecto teatral que lo secunda. Si se desea un intermedio, se hará entre la escena cuarta y la quinta, aunque lo ideal sería que se continuara con el ritmo de la obra.

Prólogo

Música sideral. Luz. Se ve el cosmos con su danza de luces, estrellas fugaces, meteoros, rocas, etc. Entra el Actor vestido de cosmonauta.

ACTOR: *(A los niños.)* Como ustedes saben, la tierra no está sola en el espacio. Hay miles y miles de estrellas, planetas, soles que iluminan otros mundos. Algunos relativamente cerca y otros muy lejanos. El espacio se estudia para conocerlo mejor. *(Confidencial.)* Pero hay quien lo hace para lograr sus malvados propósitos. Hace años, muchos años, cuando todavía había piratas, existía uno que era el más temido de todos... *(Tiembla.)* Todos le llamaban Pata de Palo, pero su nombre real era Tingo Tilingo... *(Tiembla.)* ¡Feroz pirata de los Mares del Sur! *(Entra Tingo en su barco mirando con su catalejo.)* Siempre buscaba cosas valiosas para robárselas. ¡Sobre todo le gustaba mucho el oro! Un día que espiaba el horizonte, vio una luz tremenda que cruzaba el espacio: era un cometa. *(Danza en el cielo el cometa.)* Los cometas son pura roca y hielo que viajan por el espacio. Pero este cometa en especial tenía una brillante luz dorada, que lo hacía aparecer como una gigantesca pepita de oro. *(Tingo se pone la mano detrás de la oreja y lo escucha.)* ¿Dije oro? *(Tingo asiente.)* ¿Dije que parecía una inmensa bola de... *(Tingo arma su ajetreo desesperado por ver cómo atrapa al cometa.)* ¡Nunca digan esa palabra delante de un pirata! ¡Miren cómo se ha puesto Tingo Tilingo! ¡Está tratando de agarrar el cometa! ¿Lo logrará? *(Tingo toma la cadena del ancla y la mueve sobre su cabeza, apenas el cometa pasa cerca, le tira el ancla y lo atrapa tratando de bajarlo al barco. Después de un forcejeo el cometa asciende y se lo lleva agarrado del ancla. Éste grita. El Actor se ríe.)* ¿Habrán visto pirata más tonto? ¡Y todo por el oro! Pues, sepan ustedes que Tingo Tilingo se fue con el cometa... *(Pasa el cometa con Tingo y desaparece.)* ¡Allá va! Recorriendo el espacio. Pero sepan ustedes que no estuvo durante mucho tiempo solo... *(Disparos. Música del oeste.)* ¡Pues, el desalmado cowboy Tilingo Tingo, también pensó que el cometa era de oro! *(Entra Tilingo con su lazo. Tiembla.)* ¡Era el terror del oeste! Por las tardes subía a una montaña a vigilar el paso del cometa. No había nadie como él con los lazos. Y un día... *(Entra el cometa con Tingo. Tilingo prepara el lazo y lo atrapa. Forecejea. Al final el cometa se lo lleva también. Ríe.)* ¡Y así

Tingo Tilingo y Tilingo Tingo se conocieron y anduvieron por el espacio descubriendo todos los planetas y sus cosas! Entonces fue que concibieron un diabólico plan para apoderarse de las cosas importantes en cada planeta. ¡Y debo decirles que comenzaron por nuestro planeta Tierra! Así que podemos comenzar nuestra historia diciendo: Había una vez un niño llamado René, y Canelo su perrito... *(Se va.)*

Escena primera

El jardín de René lleno de sonrientes flores, pájaros, etc. Entra Canelo ladrando detrás de los pájaros y mariposas que escapan. Huele a las flores, que ríen por las cosquillas de su nariz fría. Entra René.

RENÉ: ¡Canelo! Te he dicho que no asustes más a los pájaros. Este jardín es para todos. Deja tranquilas a los flores. *(Sale el sol.)* ¡Que día tan lindo! Regaremos las flores. *(Lo hace y las flores se bañan divertidas. Canelo persigue una oruga o mordisquea un palo o se moja con la regadera, etc. Del cielo cae una escala u otro efecto: son Tingo Tilingo con su cadena y el ancla. Y Tilingo Tingo con su lazo. Música. Una nube oculta el sol y oscurece el jardín.)*
LOS DOS:
Desde que al espacio llegamos
en busca de poder,
nunca hemos cesado
de una búsqueda emprender.

TINGO:

> De la redonda tierra,
> al quitarlos,
> los colores se acabarán
> y tendrán que comprármelos.

TILINGO:

> Con los zancos de Marte,
> todos en mi poder,
> para los marcianos
> yo seré como un rey.

LOS DOS:

> Los espejuelos de Plutón
> también nos llevaremos,
> y del lejano Urano
> las sombrillas tomaremos.
> Tingo y Tilingo
> del mundo dueños,
> Tilingo y Tingo
> a todos mandaremos... *(Ríen.)*

TINGO: ¡Un jardín! ¡Qué buen lugar para comenzar nuestra tarea! ¡Mira cuántos colores!

TILINGO: Ya estoy impaciente por llevármelos todos. ¡Y cuándo no dejemos ni un color!... *(Ríen.)*

TINGO: De cada planeta nos llevaremos algo. Todos vendrán a rogarnos que lo devolvamos. Entonces pediremos mucho dinero para hacerlo. ¡Mucho oro, oro, oro!

TILINGO: ¡Seré el mayor cowboy que ha conocido la historia! ¡Tilingo Tingo el rey del lazo! ¡El dueño del mundo!

TINGO: No, no... Dueño de medio mundo... ¿Está claro?

TILINGO: *(Molesto.)* Como tú digas... ¡Manos a la obra! *(Mueve su lazo.)*

TINGO: ¿Qué estás haciendo?

TILINGO: Voy a coger los colores.

TINGO: ¡Por mi nombre de Pata de Palo que no te dejaré! ¡Yo soy quien tiene que hacerlo! ¡Por algo soy un feroz pirata! *(Discuten. Furiosos.)* ¡Basta ya! *(Pensativo.)* Te daré... Te daré el color de...

TILINGO: ¡Los árboles! (Tingo *mueve la cabeza negándose.)* ¡El color de los helados! *(Igual.)* ¡El color de los papalotes! *(Igual.)* ¡El color de las banderas! *(Igual. Confuso.)* ¡Te los vas a coger todos! Eso no puede ser... *(Pensativo.)* ¿Comó haremos? *(Alegre.)* ¡Ya sé. *(Inesperadamente le arranca dos pelos de la barba.)*

TINGO: ¿Qué has hecho? ¿No sabes que para un pirata lo primero es su pata de palo, su parche en el ojo y su barba? Esas son las cosas que me hacen lucir muy feroz. *(Le hace una expresión terrible a los niños.)*

TILINGO: El que coja el pelo más corto, será quien se lleve los colores. (Tingo *toma uno, le da la espalda escondiéndolo, lo mira, sonríe.* Tilingo *oculta el suyo en la espalda.)* ¡Tú primero!

TINGO: ¡Tú primero! *(Juegan así hasta que le toma la mano y ve el pelo. A su vez* Tingo *le toma la suya y mira el pelo.)*

TINGO: *(Alegre.)* ¡Gané, gané!...

TILINGO: ¡Por favor, Tingo, déjame aunque sea el amarillo! Yo sé que ese color no te gusta.

TINGO: ¡Pero lo ligo con rojo y me da el naranja!

TILINGO: ¡Compláceme, Tingo Tilingo!

TINGO: ¡No puedo, Tilingo Tingo!

TILINGO: ¡Tingo Tilingo!

TINGO: ¡Tilingo Tingo!

TILINGO: ¡Está bien. Pero los zancos de Marte serán para mí.

LOS DOS:
Tingo y Tilingo
del mundo dueños,
Tilingo y Tingo
a todos mandaremos...

(Mientras Tingo *prepara su ancla para clavarla en los colores, la nube que ocultaba el sol se marcha y vuelve la luz al jardín. Ahora* Canelo *persigue un grillo,* René *limpia el jardín.* Canelo *ve un color subir y le ladra.)*

RENÉ: ¿Por qué la hierba está tan pálida? ¡Los girasoles están perdiendo el color! ¡Las mariposas son blancas! *(Viendo un color que sube.)* ¡El cielo está lleno de colores! Y, acá abajo todo se está volviendo blanco. *(Canelo sale persiguiendo el último color.)* ¡Canelo! ¡Regresa! No persigas a los colores. ¡Te vas a perder Canelo! *(Sale detrás de él. Oscuro.)*

Escena segunda

La gran pantalla de un televisor. El Locutor *con su micrófono y detrás el paisaje japonés. Sucederá todo lo que dice.*

LOCUTOR: ¡Última hora, última hora! Tenemos que anunciarles de lo último que está sucediendo en Japón. ¡En la mañana de hoy todos los abanicos se han vuelto blancos, los kimonos de las geishas perdieron su color, las hojas de té no pueden distinguirse! ¡Japón se vuelve blanco! ¡Blancooooo!... *(Oscuro. Luz a la vendedora de caramelos.)*

VENDEDORA 1: *(A los niños.)* ¡Caramelos, caramelos! ¿Quién quiere caramelos? Es inútil. ¿Quién querrá comprar un caramelo sin saber su sabor? Los verdes son de menta, los rojos de fresa, los amarillos de limón... *(Triste.)* Sólo me quedan caramelos blancos. ¡Ni yo misma sé de qué son! Desde que desaparecieron los colores no he podido vender un solo caramelo. *(Entra la Vendora 2 con su carga de reguiletes, papalotes, pelotas de playa, etc. Todo es blanco.)*

VENDEDORA 2: *(A los niños.)* ¡Reguiletes, papalotes, pelotas de playa y muchas más cosas. Las doy bien baratas. ¡Vengan y compren! También tengo juguetes. He atravesado toda la ciudad y no me compran nada.

VENDEDORA 1: ¿Quién va a querer comprar cosas sin colores? ¡Todo lo que traes parece lo mismo!

VENDEDORA 2: *(Confidencial.)* ¡Todavía me quedan unos colores! *(En la escala Tingo escucha y prepara su garfío.)* En este caja tengo escondidas unas pelotas... ¡Son de brillantes colores! Te las mostraré. *(Apenas abre la caja Tingo atrapa los colores y se los lleva. Entra Canelo ladrando y sale persiguiéndolos.)* ¡Eran las últimas que me quedaban! ¿Qué voy a vender ahora? *(Entra René.)*

RENÉ: ¿Han visto un perrito persiguiendo a los colores?

VENDEDORA 1: Se fue por allí... ¡Detrás de mis rojos, verdes y carmelitas!

VENDEDORA 2: ¡Mis amarillos, naranjas y violetas!

RENÉ: Trataré de encontrarlos. No se entristezcan. Pero ahora tengo que ir detrás de Canelo. *(Sale.)*

VENDEDORA 1: *(Marchándose muy triste.)* ¡Caramelos blancooooos!...

VENDEDORA 2: ¡Papalotes sin coloooooor!... *(Oscuro. De nuevo la pantalla del televisor.)*

LOCUTOR: Nos siguen llegando noticias de todas partes del mundo. ¡En África las cebras han perdido las rayas, en Guatemala las plumas de los quetzales han perdido su color, en Holanda los tulipanes se han vuelto blancos, en México los ocelotes ya no tienen lunares, en todo el mundo los colibríes ya no tienen plumas de colores iridicentes! Seguiremos informando. *(Oscuro.)*

Escena tercera

Un parque. Cada personaje enfrascado en lo suyo. El Estudiante rodeado de libros abiertos que son todo blancos. Sólo hay uno cerrado. Revisa algunos y se desalienta.

ESTUDIANTE: ¿Cómo voy a poder estudiar con libros que han perdido las letras? ¡Libros blancos sin dibujos, ni fotos, ni mapas, ni títulos! No podré graduarme en la escuela. *(Tomándolo.)* ¡Y sólo me queda este libro por abrir! No me atrevo. ¿Y si se escapan sus colores? *(Se escuchan claxon de autos. El desesperado* Policía *trata de guiar el tránsito, viendo perplejo como los colores de los semáforos suben al cielo.)*

POLICÍA: ¡Nadie sabe cuando tiene que detenerse, cruzar la calle o es el turno de los automóviles! Con esos semáforos sin color el tránsito tendrá que detenerse. ¡Desapareció el verde para los automóviles, el rojo de los peatones, el amarillo para esperar! ¡Nunca he visto nada igual: la ciudad sin colores! *(El* Pintor, *con sus tubos de pintura, su paleta y su pincel, trata de pintar las flores, la fuente, etc. Pero los colores ascienden.)*

PINTOR: ¡Es inútil por mucho que lo intente! Quería que el parque fuera como siempre. Ahora los niños no querrán venir a jugar. ¡Y mis pobres cuadros! ¿Cómo podré pintar un mundo sin color? ¡Se acabó el arte! *(Todos comienzan una algarabía quejándose a la vez. Entra* René.*)*

RENÉ: ¿Han visto un perrito que corre tras los colores?

ESTUDIANTE: ¡Silencio! *(Todos callan.)* ¡Este es el último libro que tiene color! Quizás si lo abro muy despacito... ¡Muy despacito! *(Todos lo rodean expectantes. Muy sigiloso.)* Así... Un poquito... Un poquito... *(Fuera del escenario* Canelo *ladra y lo sorprende y abre el libro de un tirón, el abecedario comienza a ascender. Entra* Canelo *y muerde una letra que no suelta, sube con ella. Decidido,* René *agarra la última y también asciende.)*

POLICÍA: ¡No hagas eso! Regresa.

RENÉ: Voy a ver quién se está robando los colores. Les prometo que devolveré los colores a la tierra. ¡Adióooooós! *(Desaparece. Todos se conmueven. En la escala, Tingo y Tilingo, las manos llenas de colores, ríen a carcajadas. El grupo los mira tristemente y se desbandan. Oscuro. Se ve el cosmos. Luz al Locutor sin la pantalla.)*

LOCUTOR: Sí, mis queridos amiguitos. Está confirmado que un niño llamado René y su perrito Canelo, han salido al espacio en busca de los colores perdidos. Noticias de Rusia confirman que han visto a un malvado pirata robándose los colores. En Hawai han visto a un desalmado cowboy haciendo lo mismo. No sabemos todavía por qué se roban los colores ni quiénes son. Es muy posible que nuestros amiguitos estén en peligro. *(Mira al cielo.)* ¡No podemos hacer nada porque se han alejado de la Tierra! Trataremos de mantenerlos informados. *(Oscuro.)*

Escena cuarta

Marte, el planeta rojo lleno de canales de arena. Música. Entran los Marcianos *montados en sus zancos. Estos hacen la Danza de los Zancos.*

MARCIANOS:
Hay un solo sol
y en Marte muchas lunas,
rojo es el planeta;
parece una tuna.

Los canales de Marte

de arena hay que limpiar,
nosotro los usamos
para poder viajar.

Los zancos nos evitan
nuestros pies quemar,
valen más que el oro
y las perlas del mar.

(Fuera de escena se escuchan las carcajadas de Tingo *y* Tilingo. *Después una queja o llanto.)*
MARCIANO 1: ¿Qué sucede, Klap?
MARCIANO 2: No sé, Klep. ¿Tú sabes algo Klip?
MARCIANO 3: *(Señalando hacia afuera.)* Aquéllos son Klop y Klup. ¡Y no tienen zancos! *(Se conmueven.)*
MARCIANO 1: ¡Eso nunca había sucedido! ¿Verdad, Klap, Klip?
MARCIANO 2: Es verdad lo que dice Klep. ¿No crees, Klip, que debemos ayudar a Klop y Klup con la ayuda de nosotros y Klep?
MARCIANO 3: Vamos a ellos, Klap, Klep. *(Grita.)* No se preocupen Klop y Klup que Klap, Klep y Klip van en su ayuda. *(Se arma la algarabía. Ninguno sabe por dónde salir y tropiezan, se empujan, etc. Finalmente él llega a la salida.)* ¡Klap y Klep! *(Le siguen. Entran* Tingo *y* Tilingo *sobre los zancos.* Tilingo *trae amarrados en su lazo los zancos robados.)*
TILINGO: ¿Te das cuenta los importante que son los zancos? Los marcianos los necesitan para todo: sin ellos no podrán moverse, ni limpiar los canales y cuando el sol esté fuerte... *(Ríe.)* ¡Sere-

mos los dueños de Marte! Mira a ver si nos falta alguno. ¡Tenemos que cogerlos todos! *(Tingo mira por el catalejo.)*

TINGO: ¡No lo puedo creer! ¿Te acuerdas de aquel estúpido perro que nos corría atrás?

TILINGO: Y su dueño también.

TINGO: ¡Nos vienen siguiendo! Si nos descubren, todos sabrán que fuimos nosotros los que nos robamos los colores de la Tierra.

TILINGO: Y los zancos de Marte. ¿Qué podemos hacer? *(Caminan pensativos. Se les ocurre una idea pero la rechazan. Tropiezan entre ellos y están a punto de caer.)* ¡Ya sé! *(Confidencial.)* ¡Los haremos aparecer como si fueran ellos los que se robaron los zancos! Los marcianos se pondrán furiosos. Y mientras ellos explican su inocencia. Nosotros: ¡rumbo a las sombrillas de Urano! *(Se abrazan alegres.)*

TINGO: ¡Eres un cowboy muy inteligente!

TILINGO: ¡Y tú...una pata de palo! *(Salen riendo.)*

RENÉ: *(Fuera de escena.)* Vamos a descender, Canelo. Agárrate muy bien. Ya estamos cerca. ¡Suelta las letras! ¡Ahora, Canelo! *(Caen en el escenario.)* ¿Dónde estaremos? ¡Estás lleno de arena! *(Lo sacude.)* Esto parece un inmenso desierto. *(Mirándolo.)* Hasta donde veo sólo hay arenas y rocas. *(Canelo va a unas rocas donde pueden guarecerse del sol brillante. Desde allí le ladra.)* ¡Que buen refugio has encontrado! *(Va allí y se queda dormido. Canelo escucha a los marcianos y sale tras ellos. Entran sigilosamente Tingo y Tilingo y ponen unos zancos al lado de* René. *Sonriendo alegremente, se escon-den detrás de las rocas. Entra* Canelo *seguido por los* Marcianos.)

MARCIANO 1: ¿Qué es eso Klap?

MARCIANO 2: No sé, Klep. ¿Y tú, Klip?

MARCIANO 3: Klap y Klep: ¿han visto alguna vez algo tan peludo?

MARCIANO 1: ¡Y fíjense, Klap y Klip, en lo colmi-lludo que es!

MARCIANO 2: ¡No olviden, Klep y Klip, tiene cua-tro patas! ¡Vamos a cogerlo! *(Inútilmente inten-tan cogerlo.* Canelo *despierta a* René *con los ladridos.)*

RENÉ: ¿Qué sucede? *(Los* Marcianos *se detienen y lo miran sorprendidos.)*

MARCIANO 3: ¡Klap y Klep, éste es distinto! ¿Qué será?

RENÉ: ¿Dónde estoy?

MARCIANO 1: En el planeta Marte. Yo soy Klep, éstos son Klap y Klip.

RENÉ: Mucho gusto, Klap, Klep, Klup. Yo vengo del planeta Tierra y me llamo René y este es mi perrito Canelo.

MARCIANO 2: ¿No has visto nuestros zancos?

RENÉ: Casi acabo de llegar a Marte. Sólo he visto arena, arena y arena.

MARCIANO 3: Dicen que se lo han robado unas gentes muy extrañas. *(Lo mira desconfiado.)*

MARCIANO 1: *(Igual.)* ¡Dos gentes extrañas!

MARCIANO 2: *(Igual.)* ¡Posiblemente dos gentes de la Tierra! *(*Tingo *y* Tilingo *se ríen satisfechos.* Canelo *les ladra y salen huyendo. Los* Marcianos *ven los zancos.)* ¡Klep, Klip! ¡Son nuestros zancos!

MARCIANO 3: ¿Tú no decías que no sabías nada? ¡Eres un mentiroso! Le has mentido a Klap, Klep y Klip.

MARCIANO 1: ¡Tú eres el ladrón! *(Inútilmente René trata de explicarles, pero éstos lo rodean hostilmente.* Canelo *le ladra,* René *lo sigue y salen seguidos por los coléricos* Marcianos. *En la escala* Tingo *y* Tilingo *con los zancos robados.)*

TINGO: ¡Como lo planeamos!

TILINGO: ¡Ya podemos dominar a Marte!

TINGO: ¡Ahora vamos para Urano, el planeta amarillo!

LOS DOS:
Tingo y Tilingo
del mundo dueños,
Tilingo y Tingo
a todos mandaremos...

(Salen. Brotan flores de piedras rojizas. Entra Klapklip *muy entristecida.)*

KLAPKLIP: ¿Dónde estarán mis zancos? Mientras recogía las piedrecillas de colores, alguien los ha robado. ¿Adónde podré ir sin ellos? En Marte no sabemos hacer nada sin los zancos. *(Canelo ladra fuera de escena. Asustada.)* ¿Qué es eso? *(Mira hacia afuera.)* ¡Qué extraños seres! ¡Y vienen para acá! *(Se esconde entre las flores. Entra* René *en unos zancos seguido de* Canelo.*)*

RENÉ: ¿Cómo los convenceremos de que nosotros no nos hemos robado los zancos? Nos persiguen enfurecidos. No nos han alcanzado porque no saben correr sin los zancos, pero en cualquier momento estarán aquí. Ni siquiera sabemos hacia dónde podemos ir. *(Canelo ladra hacia el escondite de Klapklip.)* ¿Qué pasa Canelo? *(Canelo va a ella que sale asustada y tropieza con* René *que cae al piso.* Klapklip *está acorralada por* Canelo.*)* No temas, Canelo no te hará nada. Ven acá, Canelo. ¿En Marte no hay perros? *(Ella niega.)* Pues, de dónde yo vengo hay muchos. *(Se enciende el planeta azul. Lo señala.)* Yo vengo de allí, de la Tierra. Mi nombre es René. ¿Y tú quién eres?

KLAPKLIP: Me llamo Klapklip y soy la recogedora de piedras.

RENÉ: ¿Para qué recoges piedras?

KLAPKLIP: Hace muchos años teníamos muchos árboles y flores. Pero todos ensuciaban el agua y la malgastaban. Tampoco cuidaban la tierra y ya ves que todo se convirtió en arena. Nunca más hemos tenido árboles ni flores. Así que las hacemos de piedrecillas de Marte. *(Se las muestra.)* No tienen perfume pero así no olvidamos que en otros lugares las flores existen. *(Triste.)* ¡Alguien ha robado mis zancos!

RENÉ: Quizás sean éstos que me encontré en medio del desierto. *(Se los muestra.)*

KLAPKLIP: Todos los zancos tienen los nombres de sus dueños para evitar confusiones.

RENÉ: *(Encuentra el nombre que lee.)* ¡Klopklop! Y tú eres Klapklip. ¡Lo siento! Pero te juro que cogeré a los que están haciendo tales fechorías. No van a seguir robando por mucho tiempo.

KLAPKLIP: ¿Qué es "robando"?

RENÉ: Tomar lo que no es tuyo sin pedirlo.

KLAPKLIP: En Marte no tenemos esa palabra. Aquí todas las cosas tienen el nombre de su dueño. Hasta las flores. *(Leyéndolas.)* Klap, Klep, Klip, Klop, Klup...

RENÉ: *(Mirando hacia afuera.)* ¡Klap, Klep, Klip, Klop, Klup! ¡Ahí vienen! Ellos creen que nosotros nos hemos robado los zancos. Si nos agarran no podremos atrapar a los verdaderos culpables.

KLAPKLIP: Eso puede ser muy peligroso. Deben ser pesonas muy malas. Ustedes solos no podrán contra ellos. Necesitan ayuda. *(Toma la cesta.)* Aquí hay cosas que los pueden ayudar.

RENÉ: Gracias Klapklip, pero no podemos perder más tiempo.

KLAPKLIP: Podría ayudarlos... Después de todo, se han robado mis zancos.

RENÉ: Les explicarás a Klap, Klep, Klip, Klop y Klup que no somos los ladrones. Nosotros le devolveremos los zancos. ¡Vamos, Canelo! *(Pone los zancos en el piso, inmediatamente el lazo de* Tilingo *los atrapa y van subiendo.* René *carga a* Canelo *y se agarra de uno. Imprevistamente* Klapklip, *con el cesto, se agarra del otro zanco y ascienden.)* ¡Tienes que quedarte! ¡No hagas eso!

KLAPKLIP: ¡Los ayudaré! Seremos tres contra esos desalmados. *(Entran los* Marcianos *que los miran asombrados.)* ¡Adiós, Klap, Klep, Klip, Klop, Klup! *(Desaparecen y se hace el oscuro sobre los consternados* Marcianos.*)*

Escena quinta

Urano, el planeta amarillo. Si se puede usar la luz negra, se verá la danza fosforecente de las sombrillas de todos tipos y colores, que al terminar salen. René, Klapklip *y* Canelo *caen del cielo.*

RENÉ: ¿Dónde estamos? *(Entra* Trestres, *que es un* Animal *con una bolsa como un canguro. Lleva en la cabeza una sombrilla como un sombrero. Todo lo que encuentra lo echa en la bolsa.)*

TRESTRES: ¡En Urano! Uno, bienvenidos, dos, que me llamo Trestres y, tres, quiénes son ustedes y, cuatro, qué hacen en Urano.

KLAPKLIP: Me llamo Klapklip y...

TRESTRES: ¡Uno no, dos no y tres no! Aquí en Urano todo lleva un número. Así que tú tienes que decir: "Uno, me llamo Klapklip, dos... ¿Ves? *(Todos se miran asombrados.)*

KLAPKLIP: *(Tímidamente.)* Uno, me llamo Klapklip, dos, soy del planeta Marte, tres, éste es René del planeta Tierra, cuatro, éste es su perro Canelo, cinco, perseguimos a unos ladrones, seis, para devolver lo robado a sus dueños, siete, y hacer que paguen sus fechorías, ocho, creemos que han venido a Urano, nueve, dinos si se han robado algo de aquí y, diez, tenemos que estar alertas.

TRESTRES: Once, yo los podría ayudar, doce, yo soy un simple Trestres de Urano, trece, los verdaderos uranos son aquellos que se acercan con las sombrillas.

RENÉ: Catorce, ¿por qué aquí todos llevan sombrillas?

TRESTRES: Quince, ellos te lo dirán. *(Entran los Uranos.)*

URANO 1: Dieciséis, ¿quiénes son ustedes?

RENÉ: Diecisiete, René del planeta Tierra, dieciocho, mi perrito Canelo, diecinueve, Klapklip del planeta Marte.

TRESTRES: Veinte, andan buscando a unos ladrones y, veintiuno, quieren saber por qué todos en Urano llevan sombrillas. *(Los* Uranos *se miran perplejos.)*

URANO 2: Veintidós, nadie nos había preguntado eso antes. Veintitrés, la verdad es que no lo sabemos. Veinticuatro, nuestros padres las usaban y... *(Aparecen* Tingo *y* Tilingo *disfrazados de magos y con la cadena y el lazo. Con gran sigilio lo escuchan todo.)*

URANOS: Veinticinco, nosotros trabajamos, ¡bajo las sombrillas! Veintiséis, se nos van los días, ¡cuidando las sombrillas! Veintiocho, discutiendo cuál es la más bonita. Veintinueve, inventando todo tipo de sombrillas. *(Las van mostrando divertidamente.)* ¡Sombrillas con bolas, sombrillas con picos, sombrillas con flecos, sombrillas con música!

TINGO: ¡Lo sabía: lo más importante de Urano son las sombrillas!

KLAPKLIP: ¡Muy bien, muy bien! ¿En qué número nos quedamos? *(René le cuenta con los dedos.)* Treinta, pero por qué las usan si no saben para qué les sirven. *(Los* Uranos *conferencian con gran algarabía. Los miren y se encogen de hombros.)*

RENÉ: Treinte y uno, vamos a ver si vemos algo por los alrededores.

TRESTRES: Treinta y dos, los acompaño. *(Salen.)*

TILINGO: ¡Nos han dejado el campo libre! No olvides nada de nuestro plan. ¡Nadie impedirá que nos adueñemos de todas las sombrillas! *(Música de magos. Aparecen en medio de una humareda.)*

TINGO: Treinta y tres, ¡han llegado a Urano los magos! Treinta y cuatro, los más reconocidos en todo el universo por sus magias. Treinta y cinco, los expertos en desaparecer y aparecer cosas. Treinta y seis, somos el Gran Abú y el Gran Baba. Treinta y siete, ¡aclamados en todos los planetas! *(Espera por* Tingo Tilingo. *Le da una patada en las nalgas.)*

TILINGO: *(Disimulando su furor. Masajeándose la patada.)* Treinta y ocho, hemos venido a Urano a enseñarles lo nunca visto, treinta y nueve, lo que se han perdido metidos siempre bajo las sombrillas. Cuarenta, ejecutaremos el gran número del lazo que hará desaparecer las sombrillas. *(Hay un rumor en los* Uranos.*)* Cuarenta y uno, no teman, que siempre devolvemos lo que hacemos desaparecer. *(Otro murmullo de alivio.)* Cuarenta y dos, ¡comenzamos! *(Redoble de tambores. Con el lazo las va enlazando. Cuando uno se queda sin sombrilla va bajo la del vecino. Sólo quedan tres.)* Cuarenta y tres, ¡la antepenúltima! Cuarenta y cuatro, ¡la penúltima!

URANOS: Cuarenta y cinco, tiene que devol-vérnoslas enseguida; no sabemos vivir sin ellas.

TILINGO: Cuarenta y seis, ¡lo sabemos! Y cuarenta y siete, ¡la última! *(Los* Uranos *se tapan los ojos y se protegen en un círculo.)*

TINGO: Cuarenta y ocho, ¡el acto ha terminado! ¡Vamos ahora a buscar los espejuelos de Plutón!

LOS DOS:
Si algo es necesario
no importa el lugar,
hazte su dueño
y a jefe has a llegar.

(Se marchan con sus carcajadas y las sombrillas dejándolos temblorosos. Canelo *entra y les ladra al cielo. Entran* René, Klapklip *y* Trestres.*)*

TRESTRES: Cuarenta y nueve, hemos llegado muy tarde.

URANOS: Cincuenta, no sabemos qué hacer sin las sombrillas. Cincuenta y uno, dicen que la luz nos hará daño y que el paisaje es muy feo.

KLAPKLIP: Cincuenta y dos, ¿cómo van a decir eso si no lo han visto? Cincuenta y tres, ¡abran los ojos y verán que no es así!

URANOS: Cincuenta y cuatro, ¡tenemos miedo!

RENÉ: Cincuenta y cinco, Trestres, quítate tu som-brilla. *(Algo temeroso, se la quita y ve que la luz no hace nada, mira en derredor maravillado.)*

TRESTRES: Cincuenta y seis, ¡es cierto, la luz no hace nada y Urano es muy bonita.

URANOS: Cincuenta y siete, no nos engañes...
*(*Klapklip *y* René *les van quitando las manos de los ojos muy gentilmente. Miran con un temor*

que se convierte en alegría.) Cincuenta y ocho, ¡no necesitamos las sombrillas!

RENÉ: Cincuenta y nueve, ustedes lo que necesitan son unos simples espejuelos para la luz.

URANO 1: Sesenta, ¡los espejuelos! Sesenta y uno, los magos dijeron que ahora iban a tomar los espejuelos de Plutón... *(Sorpresa de todos. Baja el lazo y toma el sombrero de* Trestres. *Klapklip toma a* Canelo *y se agarra a la soga, lo sigue* René *y lo sigue* Trestres. *Van ascendiendo.)*

ELLOS: Sesenta y dos, ¡hasta luego! *(Desaparecen y abajo los* Uranos *los saludan. Se dirigen a los niños alegremente.)*

URANOS:
¡Sin sombrillas,
sin sombrillas,
el mundo puedo ver,
disfrutar lo hermoso
y mucho aprender...

(Oscuro.)

Escena sexta

Plutón, el planeta de las lluvias y las nieves perpetuas donde todo el paisaje es blanco. Se escucha el relincho de un caballo. Entra el Dionos, un caballo blanco con alas y lunares triangulares. Descansa bajo un árbol cuadrado. Es que en Plutón todo tiene formas geométricas. Entra un plutoniano buscando desesperadamente, como todos ellos lleva en el pecho un emblema geométrico. Se desalienta en la búsqueda. Va a los niños.

237

PLUTONIANO 1: ¿Han visto por aquí unos espejuelos así? *(Señala el emblema.)* ¡Eran unos bellisímos espejuelos triangulares. Los necesitamos para que las constantes lluvias no nos caigan en los ojos. Sin ellos no sabemos qué hacer. Será un gran desastre para Plutón. ¿Quién puede querer nuestros espejuelos? *(Entran los otros plutonianos.)* Ellos tampoco saben.

PLUTONIANO 2: Quizás han visto los míos... *(A los niños. Señala su emblema.)* Eran unos espejuelos cuadrados...

PLUTONIANO 3: *(Igual.)* Eran unos espejuelos rectangulares...

PLUTONIANO 1: También los había redondos, pentagonales... ¡Sólo de pensarlo me pongo tan triste! *(*Todos *se abrazan.)*

PLUTONIANOS: ¿Qué podremos hacer sin nuestros espejuelos? *(Se marchan llorando. Entran* René, Canelo, Klapklip y Trestres.*)*

RENÉ: Alguien llora.

DIONOS: Es que se han robado todos los espejuelos de Urano.

KLAPKLIP: Llegamos tarde.

TRESTRES: Uno, qué haremos ahora. Dos, porque ya éste es el último planeta.

DIONOS: ¡Que extraño hablas! ¿Quién eres?

TRESTRES: Tres, me llamo Trestres y soy del planeta Urano.

RENÉ: Yo soy René del planeta Tierra y éste es mi perro Canelo. *(*Canelo *ladra.)*

KLAPKLIP: Yo soy Klapklip del planeta Marte.

DIONOS: Pues yo soy Dionos de Plutón. *(Relincha.)*

RENÉ: Te pareces a los caballos. Lo único que en la tierra no tienen alas, ni esos triángulos en el cuerpo.

DIONOS: Es que aquí todo tiene una forma... Las rocas son redondas, los árboles cuadrados, las nubes triangulares...

TRESTRES: Cuatro, ¿tú sabes algo de quién se robó los espejuelos?

DIONOS: Pues, vi un cometa que se iba cargado de cosas.

RENÉ: ¿Con colores? *(Dionos asiente.)*

KLAPKLIP: ¿Con zancos? *(Igual.)*

TRESTRES: Cinco, con sombrillas. *(Igual.)*

DIONOS: Y hasta creo que con nuestros espejue-los... *(Entran los* Plutonianos.*)*

PLUTONIANOS: ¿Nuestros espejuelos?

RENÉ: Son unos malvados que se están robando las cosas de los planetas.

KLAPKLIP: Quieren convertirse en los dueños del universo, ser ricos y poderosos.

PLUTONIANOS: ¿Entonces hemos perdido nues-tros espejuelos para simpre? ¡Cuando comience la lluvia no podremos ver!

TRESTRES: Seis, y nosotros que pensabámos atra-parlos. Ya no podremos hacer nada aunque seamos muchos.

RENÉ: Si nos unimos podremos vencerlos. Ahora lo más importante es saber dónde se esconden.

DIONOS: Yo lo sé. El cometa me pareció muy sospechoso y volé detrás de él por un rato. Yo sé dónde se detuvo.

KLAPKLIP: ¿Y cómo llegaremos allá?

DIONOS: ¡Yo los llevaré! *(Alegría general.)* Tienen que agarrarse bien, pues es algo lejos.

PLUTONIANOS: ¿Nos devolverán nuestros espejuelos?

RENÉ: Si todos cooperamos, estoy seguro que lo lograremos. *(Todos se montan sobre el Dionos que comienza su vuelo. Abajo los Plutonianos los despiden alegres. Oscuro.)*

Escena séptima

El planeta Saturno. Sus anillos están llenos de las cosas robadas. Por todas partes hay cárteles: "NO PASAR," "PROHIBIDO COGER NADA," "PROPIEDAD DE TINGO TILINGO," "PROPIEDAD DE TILINGO TINGO," etc. Entran todos.

TRESTRES: Cuatro, miren allí: ¡los colores, los zancos, sombrillas, espejuelos!

KLAPKLIP: ¡Han convertido a Saturno en el planeta de los cosas robadas! ¡Malvados! Jamás los hubiéramos encontrado si no fuera por Dionos que los siguió.

RENÉ: Debemos tener cuidado. Deben andar cerca.

DIONOS: Podemos coger todas las cosas y marcharnos antes de que lleguen. Pero debemos ser muy cuidadosos. *(El Grupo va hacia los objetos.)*

KLAPKLIP: ¡Esperen! Aquí hay un cártel: "El que entre aquí será apresado." ¡Es una trampa! *(Canelo ladra a Tingo y Tilingo que estaban escondidos y halan un lazo y cae una red que los atrapa. Canelo se escapa.)*

TINGO: ¿Se creían más inteligentes que Tingo Tilingo y Tilingo Tingo? Tomamos precauciones por si metían las narices por aquí. ¿Ven qué caro les costó estarnos siguiendo y oponerse a nuestros planes?

TILINGO: Para que cada planeta recupere sus cosas, tendrán que nombrarnos sus gobernantes y darnos todas las riquezas que posean. ¡Seremos los dueños del mundo!

LOS DOS: *(Bailando.)*
Tingo y Tilingo
del mundo dueños,
Tilingo y Tingo
a todos mandaremos.

RENÉ: No van a salirse con la suya. Tendrán que devolver todo lo que han robado.

KLAPKLIP: Y serán castigados...

LOS DOS: ¡Ay, qué miedo!

TRESTRES: Seis, que los venceremos porque estamos unidos.

TINGO: ¿Cómo van a unirse si todos son tan diferentes? Y cada uno viene de un lugar distinto. Ninguno es igual al otro.

DIONOS: Eso no impide que nos unamos para luchar contra ustedes. Solamente lucimos distintos pero todos somos iguales.

RENÉ: Y nos respetamos como somos.

TINGO: Pues yo sólo acepto a los piratas como yo.

TILINGO: Y a los vaqueros como yo.

KLIPKLAP: Pero el mundo también está compuesto de gentes diferentes. No hay que odiar a los que no son como nosotros.

TILINGO: ¡Basta ya! Estamos muy ocupados con-
tando nuestras riquezas. ¿Qué hacemos con
ellos, Tingo Tilingo? *(Caminan pensativos de un
lado a otro. Chocan entre sí, etc.)*

KLAPKLIP: ¡Tengo un plan! *(Hablan entre ellos y
al final asienten.)*

TINGO: ¡Ya sé! ¡Vamos a buscar el ancla! ¡Volvere-
mos a agarrar el cometa y los pondremos a ellos
bien amarraditos!

TILINGO: ¿Y andarán por los cielos como nosotros?
¡Qué Pata de Palo tan inteligente! Ahora sabrán
lo que es andar de un sitio a otro. Nadie podrá
rescatarlos. ¡Vamos a buscar el ancla!

KLAPKLIP: ¡Un momento! Si me dejan libre, les
mostraré las minas de diamantes rojos que hay
en Marte.

TINGO: Nunca he visto diamantes rojos.

KLAPKLIP: Busquen en mi cesta. *(Van a la cesta y
toman las piedrecillas rojas que llenan de fulgor
el lugar.)*

TILINGO: ¡Son míos!

TINGO: ¡Son míos! *(Discuten y forcejean.)*

KLAPKLIP: En Marte hay para los dos: ¡montañas
de diamantes!

LOS DOS: ¿Dónde? ¿Cómo se llega allí? ¿En qué
parte de Marte?

KLAPKLIP: Yo solo lo sé. Los llevaré allí si me
zafan. *(Los dos conferencian.)*

TINGO: Está bien. Irás con nosotros. Pero éstos se
van en el cometa.

TILINGO: *(A los niños.)* Y cuando tengamos todos
los diamantes, a ella también la pondremos en

el cometa. *(Sacan a* Klapklip *y mientras anudan la red ella va a un extremo.)*

KLAPKLIP: *(Burlona.)* ¡Tingo Tilingo y Tilingo Tingo! *(Les hace una señal y sale. Éstos salen gritando detrás de ella. Entra* Canelo.*)*

RENÉ: ¡Desata esas sogas, Canelo! *(Lo hace.)*

DIONOS: ¿Qué hacemos ahora? Hay que pensar en algo mientras Klapklip los entretiene.

RENÉ: Hay que buscar la manera de atraparlos.

TRESTRES: Siete, yo puedo ayudarlos. *(Saca distintas cosas de su bolsa hasta que encuentra la fruta.)* Ocho, ésta es una fruta de Urano llamada Nuevediez. Su olor es tan fuerte que inmoviliza al que la huele. La pondré aquí para que la encuentren. Nos haremos los que seguimos atados.

DIONOS: ¡Ya atraparon a Klapklip! ¡Regresemos bajo la red! *(Lo hacen. Entra* Tilingo *con la cadena y el ancla.* Tingo *trae a* Klapklip.*)*

TINGO: Por engañarnos te irás con ellos en el cometa. Nosotros sabremos encontrar los diamantes en Marte.

TRESTRES: Nueve, pero no podrán encontrar al Nuevediez: la fruta del oro.

LOS DOS: ¿La fruta del oro?

TRESTRES: Diez, allí hay una. Es la fruta que en vez de semillas tiene una piedra de oro. Los árboles están cuajados de Nuevediez, hay por todas partes, llenos de oro, oro, oro... *(*Tingo *se lanza a cogerla, pero* Tilingo *también y forcejean, de pronto la parten.)*

RENÉ: ¡Aléjate, Klapklip! *(Estos son envueltos en un humo que los deja paralizados. Todos salen debajo de la red y los atrapan con ella.)*

DIONOS: ¡Hemos triunfado! *(Todos van a los objetos.)* ¡Los espejuelos de Plutón!

TRESTRES: ¡Las sombrillas de Urano!

KLAPKLIP: ¡Los zancos de Marte! *(Miran a René.)* ¿Por qué no coges los colores?

RENÉ: He pensado que como Marte es todo rojo, quizás le pueda dar algunos colores de la Tierra.

KLAPKLIP: Y yo pudiera darte algunos zancos para que los niños jueguen.

TRESTRES: Quizás los espejuelos de Plutón sean mejor para el sol.

DIONOS: ¡Y las sombrillas mejor para la lluvia! *(En una alegría general hacen los trueques.)*

RENÉ: Ahora cada uno regresará a su planeta. Veremos qué cástigo le dan a estos malvados. *(A los niños.)* ¡Y colorín colorado el cuento se está acabando! *(Oscuro.)*

Escena final

Una luz al Locutor.

LOCUTOR: ¡Noticias de última hora confirman que ha caído una lluvia de sombrillas sobre Plutón, una de espejuelos sobre Urano, una de colores sobre Marte y aquí en la tierra están lloviendo zancos! Dicen que traen a la Tierra a los malvados Tingo Tilingo y Tilingo Tingo para castigarlos. ¡Los mantendremos informados! *(Luz a los* Plutonianos *con las sombrillas, los* Uranos *con los espejuelos, los* Marcianos *con los colores y los* Personajes Terrícolas *con los zancos. Por el cielo pasa el cometa que todos saludan.* Dionos, Trestres, Klapklip *y* René *van a los suyos.)*

RENÉ: ¡Gracias, Klapklip, Trestres, y Dionos! *(*Canelo *ladra.)* ¡Gracias, Canelo! *(*Todos *se intercambian las gracias. Entran* Tingo Tilingo *y* Tilingo Tingo *con trajes carcelarios y arrastrando unas bolas de hierro. Pasan barriendo y desaparecen. Música.* Todos *bailan.)*

TODOS:
Unidos, unidos, unidos,
todos los iguales
y los diferentes,
con un solo brazo
habremos vencido.

RENÉ: Y ahora sí amiguitos…

TODOS: ¡Colorín colorado este cuento se ha terminado!

La lente maravillosa

de

Emilio Carballido

La lente maravillosa
de Emilio Carballido

Melodrama para niños muy pequeños

Personajes

EL ANCIANO
MARÍA
LOLA
PACO
JUAN
MICROBIO NO IDENTIFICADO
OTRO MICROBIO
BACILO
COCO
AMIBA

Un jardin público, un rincón del mismo jardín y la pantalla para proyecciones.

Primer acto

Jardín público: fuente grande al fondo, árboles, plantas, bancas.

Un anciano estrafalario avanza a primer término y se dirige al público.

VIEJO: Amiguitos, muy buenos días. He venido para contarles cuentos maravillosos, pero no sé por cuál empezar. Por supuesto, pienso ilustrarlos, sé hacer algunos trucos que tal vez... *(Algo le molesta en el cuello, se saca una interminable choricera de mascadas.)* No me refería a esto, claro. *(Hace aparecer un huevo sin querer, lo guarda en la bolsa.)* Lo que pasa es que hay un cuento muy bueno, del árbol que camina... *(Pasa caminando un árbol.)* y da dulces en vez de frutas. Mírenlo, allá va. *(Corta algunos dulces, los tira a los niños.)* Pero hay un cuento que a mí me gusta más. *(Tose.)* ¿No quieren acercarse algunos, para que me oigan mejor? Anden, con confianza. *(De la luneta suben Paco, María, Lola y Juan.)*

MARÍA: ¿De veras podemos sentarnos aquí?

VIEJO: Sí, hijita. Por supuesto. *(Severo.)* Pero quietos y sin hacer ruido. *(Se sientan los niños.)* Les voy a contar un cuento de animales, y de unos animales ¡terribles!

JUAN: *(Contento.)* ¡Leones, tigres!

PACO: ¡Pan, pan, pan! *(Disparando.)*

VIEJO: ¡No! Voy a hablar de unos animales tan chicos, tan chicos que nadie los podía ver, y tan malvados que se dedicaban a hacer sufrir a todos los niños del mundo.

LOLA: ¿Y nadie podía verlos?

VIEJO: Nadie.

LOS CUATRO: *(Decepcionados.)* Aaah. *(Se ven entre sí.)*

PACO: Pues si no vamos a ver a los animales... *(Quedo.)* Vámonos.

JUAN: *(Quedo.)* Sí, vámonos. *(Codazo a las niñas.)*

PACO: Creo que...que nos habla la mamá de Lola, sí, oigan. *(Los empuja.)* Corran. *(Salen corriendo tres de ellos, menos Paco, que se retrasa.)*

VIEJO: Bueno, pues estos niños no verán los animales.

PACO: *(Frena.)* Ah, ¿pero vamos a verlos?

VIEJO: ¡Claro!

PACO: ¿Pues no decía usted que no podían verse?

VIEJO: No pueden verse nada más con los ojos, pero yo soy dueño de unas cosas...

PACO: ¿Qué cosas?

VIEJO: ¡Lentes!

PACO: ¿Lentes?

VIEJO: ¡Lentes maravillosas para ver lo invisible! Y entonces, aunque esos animales son tan pequeños, tan pequeños, ¡uno puede verlos!

PACO: ¿Y me los va a enseñar?

VIEJO: Si tú quieres... ¡Ara zalila balún! *(Relámpagos, truenos, oscuridad. Descendió la pantalla para proyecciones. Inmediatamente se proyecta lo que el diálogo va indicando.)*

PACO: Ay, ¿qué es eso que se ve ahí?

VIEJO: ¿Ves qué grande se ve? Más grande que tú. Pues eso...¡es una gota de agua! Mi lente hace que se vea así de grande.

PACO: ¿Una gota de agua?

VIEJO: Eso. Y adentro de una gota, ¡mira todas las cosas que puede hacer!

PACO: ¡Sí! ¡Veo figuritas! ¡Pero muy chicas!

VIEJO: Pues imagínate qué tan chicas serán, que están adentro de una gota de agua. Ahora, vas a ver al fin una de esas figuritas, cómo la vuelvo grande.

PACO: ¡Ah! ¿Y qué es eso?

VIEJO: Ese es uno de los animales invisibles, por que es tan chico que nadie lo puede ver con los simples ojos. ¿Ves cómo lo hace grande mi lente?

PACO: ¿Ese es un animal?

VIEJO: Sí. También este otro. ¿Sabes cómo se llaman?

PACO: ¿Cómo?

VIEJO: ¡Microbios!

PACO: ¿Y de veras son malos?

VIEJO: Muy malos. Pueden ser más peligrosos que los leones.

PACO: ¡Qué lástima que no vinieron mis amigos!

VIEJO: Culpa tuya. ¡Alibán zapón pan! *(Truenos, relámpagos, oscuridad. Otra vez el jardín.)*

PACO: Ay, ya volvimos al jardín.

VIEJO: Ya.

PACO: Oiga, señor: ¿Y no podría prestarme una lente de esas maravillosas?

VIEJO: ¿Y para qué la quieres?

PACO: Pues haría yo crecer a los microbios, y se los enseñaría a mis amigos.

VIEJO: ¿Y no te da miedo que crezcan?

PACO: Pues no. Fueran leones…

VIEJO: Pues tú sabes. Te la puedo prestar un rato, pero ten cuidado. Si quieres nada más verlos tú, basta con que veas a través de ella, pero si quieres que todo mundo los vea, tienes que hacer que pase un poco de luz a través el vidrio, y ante tus propios ojos crecerán los microbios. *(De una bolsa bordada saca una enorme lente, con largo mango.)* Toma, y no la vayas a romper. Bueno, tengo prisa. Y te repito, ten cuidado cómo la usas. *(Sale.)*

PACO: Gracias, señor. Gracias ¡Oiga! ¿Por qué dice que debo tener cuidado? ¡Ya se fue! ¿Y cómo se usará esto? *(Entra Juan.)*

JUAN: ¿Qué pasó? ¿No que no querías oír al viejo?

PACO: ¡Me enseñó cosas muy bonitas! ¡Vi los animales invisibles!

JUAN: ¿Pues no decía que no se podían ver?

PACO: Pero se ven, con unas lentes. Y me prestó ésta, que los hace crecer.

JUAN: A poco.

PACO: ¡Palabra! Bueno, eso me dijo él.

JUAN: ¡Te ha de haber engañado!

PACO: Pues... *(Desconfía.)* Dice que si hacemos que pase la luz... Mira, aquí está dando el sol. Podemos sujetarla aquí, por el mango... A ver, que caiga la luz en la fuente.

JUAN: ¿Qué pasó? No se ve nada. Ningún animal aparece.

PACO: Pues no. Creo que... Oye, ¿qué es eso que se mueve ahí? *(Un microbio se asoma y desaparece dentro de la fuente.)*

JUAN: ¿Adónde?

PACO: Se me figuró... *(Están de espaldas a la fuente, muy cerca.)* Pues será que no hay bastante sol. Mira, le da muy bien... *(Dos microbios se asoman y estiran las manos para agarrarlos. Los pierden por milímetros.)*

JUAN: Creo que no está bien sujeta. Ayúdame. *(La arreglan, retroceden acercándose a la fuente. Otra vez van a pescarlos los microbios, que ahora son tres.)*

PACO: Yo creo que esta lente no sirve de nada.

JUAN: Te lo dije.

PACO: A ver si moviéndola para allá. *(Otra vez se les escapan a los microbios, que se esconden de nuevo.)*

PACO: Pues no. No se ve nada. A no ser que estén en el agua. A ver.

JUAN: A ver. *(Alarido y carrera, porque hora sí casi los pescan, y de frente, los microbios, que surgieron repentinamente y con las garras listas.)*

PACO: ¡Esos han de ser!

JUAN: ¡Qué feos son!

PACO: ¡Por poco nos pescan!

JUAN: ¡No te asomes! ¡Míralos! Son tan chiquititos que caben muchos en una gota de agua, pero ahora la lente los hizo crecer. *(Los microbios emergen descaradamente. Son cuatro o más si se puede. Son profundamente malvados y pérfidos. Emiten risitas crueles.)*

BACILO: ¿Adónde rayos se nos escaparon esos niños?

AMIBA: ¡Ya casi los habíamos pescado!

COCO: Pero han de regresar, siempre regresan.

AMIBA: ¿Tú crees que beban agua de la fuente?

MICROBIO: ¡Claro! ¡Les encanta beber agua puerca!

AMIBA: ¡Bravo! ¡Los enfermaré! ¡Tendrán cólicos y calentura! ¡Tal vez hasta los purguen, o los inyecten! *(Ríe a carcajadas.)*

BACILO: ¡Mira aquellas dos! ¡Están haciendo tortas de lodo! ¿Tú crees que se laven después las manos?

COCO: ¡Qué va!

MICROBIO: ¡Ojalá que coman dulces con las manos sucias! Porque así estaré listo para acabármelos.

COCO: ¡Tal vez se hagan raspones y se los dejen llenos de mugre! Ahí estaré yo, para hincharlos.

(Gritos generales de entusiasmo.)

Cantan todos: (Marcha.)

> Somos los microbios
> y venimos a enfermar
> a esos niños sucios
> que no se quieren lavar.
> ¡No se laven nunca,
> no se laven nunca!
> ¡Cuando estén enfermos,
> cuánto vamos a gozar!

(Marchan gozosos, hacen gestos amenazadores. Luego, invitan.)

(Con perfidia.)

Vengan, niños, vengan,
en la fuente han de beber,
aunque esté muy turbia,
ya que tienen mucha sed.
¡Viva el agua sucia!
¡Viva el agua sucia!
Y en las uñas largas
nos podemos esconder.

*(Marchan triunfalmente, riendo y tropezándose,
llenos de maldad.)*

Agua de manguera
también la pueden probar.
¡Coman muchos dulces,
con las manos sin lavar!
¡Somos los microbios,
somos los microbios,
y a todos los niños
los queremos enfermar!

*(Entre gritos y mutuas felicitaciones terminan su
numerito.)*

COCO: Creo que estoy en magníficas condiciones.
Me siento capaz de hincharles manos y pies.

AMIBA: Yo voy a provocarles cólicos tan fuertes que
los enfermitos se van a retorcer como lombrices.

BACILO: Yo los voy a hacer toser sin descanso,
hasta que escupan el esqueleto por lo boca.

MICROBIO: ¡Nadie va a poder detenernos!

PACO: ¿Y ahora qué vamos a hacer? El viejo tonto
me dio la lente para hacerlos crecer, pero no me
dijo cómo defenderme de ellos.

COCO: ¿Oyeron? Creo que un niño anda por aquí.

JUAN: ¿Ves idiota? ¡Ya te oyeron!

BACILO: ¡Son dos!

PACO: Pues ya te oyeron a ti también.

MICROBIO: Listos para el asalto.

AMIBA: Dice que no sabe cómo defenderse. *(Ríen todos a carcajadas. Van acercándose lentamente. Paco y Juan corren atontados, son asaltados, huyen finalmente a la luneta y se esconden entre los asientos. Lentamente, empiezan a descender los microbios.)*

COCO: ¡Mira cuántos niños!

BACILO: ¡Y allí está uno que tiene las manos sucias!

AMIBA: ¡Mira qué uñas tan largas tiene aquélla!

MICROBIO: ¡Hay muchos, muchos, todos para nosotros! *(Se van acercando más a los niños del público.)*

COCO: ¿A cuál vamos a atacar primero? *(Aparecen en el foro María y Lola; vienen muy sucias.)*

LOLA: ¿Qué pasó? ¡Juaaan! ¡Paaaacoooo!

MARÍA: ¡Si no vienen, nos vamos! ¿No quieren hacer tortas de lodo?

LOLA: ¡Ya no se escondan!

COCO: *(Ruge.)* ¡Mira qué delicia!

AMIBA: ¡Esas son las más sucias!

TODOS: ¡A ellas! *(Corren y caen encima de ellas.)*

MARÍA Y LOLA: ¡Ay mamacita linda! ¡Nos están llevando los monstruos! *(Se las llevan arrastrando. Ellas gritan.)*

PACO: ¡Se llevaron a María y a Lola!

JUAN: ¿Y ahora qué hacemos?

PACO: ¡Hay que buscar al viejito, para que nos ayude a rescatarlas! *(Salen corriendo por el foro.)*

Telón

Segundo acto

Cuadro primero

Ante el telón, sentado en el filo del proscenio, el Viejo lee atentamente un libro. Entran corriendo Paco *y* Juan.

PACO: ¡Señor, señor! ¡Vinieron los microbios!...

JUAN: ...¡Y se llevaron a mi hermana!...

PACO: ...¡Y a una amiguita de ella!

VIEJO: ¿Cómo es posible? *(Se levanta.)* A ver, cuéntame. ¿Usaste la lente maravillosa?

PACO: ¡Sí! ¡Y salieron unos microbiotes enormes!

JUAN: ¡Nos corretearon!

PACO: ¡Y luego se llevaron a María y a Lola!

VIEJO: Dime qué aspecto tenían, para saber con qué armas vamos a combatirlos.

PACO: ¡Eran...muy feos!

JUAN: ¡Grandes! ¡Con patas!

PACO: Uno tenía muy pocas patas. Parecía como...una sabanota.

JUAN: Pero había otro que tenía muchas.

VIEJO: Vamos a ver si los reconocen. Voy a enseñarles algunos cuantos. *(Se abre el telón. Pasan las proyecciones con mucha rapidez.)* ¿Eran como éstos?

NIÑOS: ¡Nooo!

VIEJO: ¿Como éstos?

NIÑOS: ¡Nooo!

PACO: ¡Como ésos eran, como ésos eran!

VIEJO: *(Como los policías cuando el criminal es reconocido.)* ¡Ahh! Estos son amibas, viven en el agua sucia y dan horrorosos dolores de barriga cuando te los bebes. ¿Y no había de estos otros?

NIÑOS: ¡Sí, de ésos también!

VIEJO: Estos se esconden en los rasguños sucios, y en los raspones, para hincharte los brazos y las piernas!

NIÑOS: ¡También había de esos otros!

VIEJO: ¡Este es de los peores! Es muy pequeño y se llama bacilo de Koch. Se esconde en todas partes, da la tuberculosis y pone a los niños flacos y moribundos. Vive en el polvo de los jardines, donde la gente escupe. ¡Pero hay que apresurarse, para salvar a sus amigas!

PASO: ¿Y por qué no me dijo cómo desaparecerlos?

VIEJO: ¡No te dije! Es que a veces me distraigo. Soy distraído. Bastaba con que pusieras la lente al revés. ¡Vamos a salvar a las niñas! ¡Han de tenerlas en algún rincón húmedo y oscuro del jardín! Pero antes, tenemos que estar muy limpios; vamos a comprar cepillos de dientes y a lavarnos la boca, luego las manos, y hay que ponernos ropa limpia. ¡Aprisa! ¡Ah! ¡Y hay que cortarse las uñas! ¡Sólo así no podrán hacernos nada! *(Salen corriendo. Oscuridad.)*

Cuadro segundo

Un rincón del jardín. Especie de cueva muy baja, formada por ramas. Las niñas amarradas. Los microbios las observan.

LOLA: *(Gime.)* Señor, señor, no sea malo, deje que nos vayamos.

COCO: No soy señor. Soy microbio. *(Muy grosero.)*

AMIBA: Bueno. ¿Quién empieza? ¡Yo, mano!

COCO: Yo tras.

BACILO: Yo cola.

OTRO MICROBIO: Y luego sigo yo.

COCO: ¿Qué les vas a hacer tú?

AMIBA: *(Cruel.)* ¿No tienen sed, niñitas?

LOLA Y MARÍA: Sí, seño...digo...

MARÍA: Sí, Don Microbio. Mucha sed.

AMIBA: Pues les voy a dar de beber... ¡¡¡agua de la fuente!!! Se enfermarán de cólicos y calentura. *(Ríe a carcajadas.)*

COCO: Jugaron con lodo, ¿no? Pues yo no voy a dejar que se laven las manos, hasta que se les hinchen. *(Carcajadas.)*

BACILO: *(Feliz.)* Y yo les voy a dar dulces y pan... ¡para que coman con las manitas sucias, y luego yo entre a sus pulmoncitos con el pan, y las haga toser y toser, hasta reventarlas! *(Carcajadas.)*

MICROBIO: ¡Y yo las voy a tener despeinadas y con la ropa sucia, hasta que se llenen de granos! *(Carcajadas.)*

TODOS: *(Bailan y cantan en torno a ellas.)*
¡Somos los microbios,

somos los microbios,
y a todos los niños
los queremos enfermar!

VIEJO: *(Fuera de escena.)* ¡Oigo cantos y gritos, creo que aquí están!

MARÍA Y LOLA: ¡Aquí estamos, aquí estamos! *(Entra el* Viejo, *vestido con albeante bata médica;* Paco y Juan, *muy limpios, detrás.)*

COCO: ¡Qué se han creído! ¡Estas niñas son nuestras, por sucias!

PACO: ¡Aquí traigo un palo muy bueno, que limpiamos con agua, jabón y alcohol, para pegarles con él!

JUAN: ¡Y yo traigo otro!

AMIBA: ¡Al ataque! *(Atacan, pero es como si un aura invisible protegiera a los niños.)*

MICROBIO: ¡No les puedo hacer nada!

COCO: ¡Están demasiado limpios!

AMIBA: ¡Este viejo está más limpio que ninguno! *(Los niños les dan de palos y los hacen correr.)*

VIEJO: No los dejen ir. Yo voy a desatar a estas niñas y a lavarles las manos. ¡Alcáncenlos! *(Persecución de microbios por la luneta. En el escenario, salen el* Viejo *y las* Niñas. *Cambio a jardín.)*

MICROBIOS: ¡Pido paz, pido paz, pido paz!

JUAN Y PACO: ¡Yo te voy a dar paz!

MICROBIOS: ¡A la fuente! ¡A la fuente! *(Corren y se meten ahí.)*

PACO: ¡Pronto, a darle vuelta a la lente! *(Le dan vuelta y los microbios desaparecen.)*

JUAN: ¡Se fueron!

PACO: Yo creo que ahí están todavía, pero invisibles, como eran antes.

VIEJO: *(Entrando.)* Muy cierto. Siguen ahí, y así pequeñitos e invisibles son más peligrosos todavía, porque no nos damos cuenta de su presencia.

JUAN: ¿Y Lola y María?

VIEJO: Están acabando de asearse, para que ningún microbio pueda hacerles nada. *(Entran Lola y María.)*

LOLA Y MARÍA: ¡Miren qué limpias estamos!

LOLA: ¡Ahora sí, que vengan los microbios!

LOS 4 NIÑOS: *(Cantan.)*
Como somos niños limpios
los microbios no vendrán;
en sus charcos y en el lodo
humillados quedarán. *(Bailan.)*

TODOS: ¡Humillados quedarán!

VIEJO:
No bebo agua de la llave
porque me puedo enfermar.
Con poner a hervir el agua
los microbios morirán. *(Baila.)*

TODOS:
¡Los microbios morirán!
Aunque chicos e invisibles
los microbios ahí están,
con limpieza y con cuidado
nada me puede pasar. *(Bailan.)*
¡Con limpieza y con cuidado
nada me puede pasar!
Pero ahora los conozco,

no me pueden engañar,
si estoy limpio y bien peinado
siempre sano voy a estar! *(Bailan.)*
¡Siempre sano voy a estar!
(Ritardando.)
Los microbios derrotados
ya no hay nada que contar,
colorín y colorado,
el cuento se va acabar.

Telón

Biographies and Background Information

Biographies and Background Information

Emilio Carballido

Emilio Carballido is one of Mexico's most distinguished playwrights. Born in 1925 in Veracruz, he graduated from the National Autonomous University of Mexico in 1949 and began writing, directing and teaching theater in Mexico's leading universities and cultural institutions. His awards include national and international prizes for his plays and prestigeous fellowships from the Rockefeller Foundation and the Centro Mexicano de Escritores. His numerous plays have been staged and published internationally.

"La lente maravillosa" is a short, brilliant example of how to make the teaching of science, in this case hygiene, exciting and pleasurable. Carballido's script shows how to channel a child's natural curiosity and imagination towards learning science and language with great pleasure. The editor has seen this script in action in one of the theaters of the Seguro Social in Mexico, and has witnessed a full auditorium of spellbound children and adults. The "lente maravillosa" refers to the microscope.

Roy Conboy

Roy Conboy is a Chicano-Irish writer and director whose plays have been produced by El Teatro de la Esperanza in San Francisco, the Guadalupe Cultural Arts Center in San Antonio, Teatro Latino of Minnesota, PCPA Theaterfest in Santa Maria, California, Cucucuevez Multi-Cultural Theatre in Santa Ana, California, Cypress Community College, Mesa Community College, Chabot Community College, Rancho Santiago College and San Francisco State University.

In addition, his plays have been seen in workshops or staged readings at The Mark Taper Forum, South Coast Repertory, The American Conservatory Theatre, The Seattle Group Theatre, The Bay Area Playwright Festival, Latin American Theatre Artists, The Miracle Theatre Group/Teatro Milagro, The Audrey Skirball-Kenis Theatre and INTAR.

In 1991 he was the recipient of a Fellowship for Playwrights from the National Endowment for the Arts. He has been an Associated Artist of The Magic Theatre in San Francisco and the Director of the Isadora Aquirre Playwrighting Lab for El Teatro de la Esperanza. He is an Associate Professor at San Francisco State University and a founding member and Artistic Associate of the multi-cultural theatre company, Cucucuevez. He has also served as the General Manager and Casting Director of the Grove Shakespeare Festival in Garden Grove and as the director of the New Plays and Players Workshop at Rancho Santiago College in Santa Ana.

His plays for children include "¡Nunca Soñar Mas!" / "No More Dreams!," "Hot Tamale!" / "¡Tamale Caliente!," "La Caja Misteriosa" / "The Mystery Box," and "Happy Birthday, Angel." His plays for adults include "When El Cucui Walks," "Dancing With the Missing," "Camino Confusión" / "Confusion Street" and "Buscando América" / "Seeking America."

"El Canto del Roble" / "The Song of the Oak" is a bilingual fable in which a self-appointed detective learns the mystery of what goes into the making of oak leaves. It is a beautiful, lyrical play in which children can enjoy themselves playing the various forms of life and singing the songs that the various forms of life sing. The story is told lightly, humorously and suspensefully.

The author, Roy Conboy, indicates that the play is written for four actors. This means that the actors can change roles in full view of the audience, thus providing theatricality by permitting the audience to guess how the metamorphosis from one character to another will work out. Also, the fact that the changes can occur in full view of the audience does not restrict the action to the traditional proscenium stage, which separates the audience from the actors. It permits for various kinds of staging, and can create an atmosphere of strong audience participation through actor-audience contact. For example, while the change of character goes on, the main actor can open a dialogue with the audience about what kind of effect it expects. There are many options, among them the fact that the director can choose to use as large a number of woodland characters as he/she wishes without marring the purpose of the script. It is a very versatile script.

José Gaytán

José Gaytán is a native of Monterrey, México. He came to the United States as a young man, was schooled here, became a communications expert for the telephone company and served in the Army. "Fred Menchaca and His Burro, Filemón" is an actor's monologue, and was never intended as a literary piece. It was written by the actor, Gaytán, for himself, and presented with considerable success to many school children all over Corpus Christi, Texas. The playwright, José G. Gaytán, came into acting by way of his stint with the Army in France. His first roles were in plays by Moliere, which rely heavily on the actor's ability and training to make the most of simple situations. This play has a simple plot. The actor tells children the story of how Fred Menchaca, a *rancherito*, went to France and was exposed to a new way of behavior, but found, when he returned, that those back home were not ready for what he had learned. He applies the same simple wisdom of dealing with his burro: consider whom you're dealing with before acting. A cross cultural experience three ways: involving Mexicans, French and burros.

José Gaytán has written other short pieces, one entitled "Filemón," the other "Benito Juárez." In the latter he explains the meaning of the 5 de mayo celebration. In South Texas many people celebrate 5 de mayo, but most of them do not know why. He has held adults enthralled by his performance of Benito Juárez's explanation of that commemorative holiday.

Alvan Colón Lespier

Alvan Colón Lespier is a New Yorker of Puerto Rican descent. He is at present associate artistic director of the theater group, Pregones, where he has been since 1981. Before that he was co-founder of the Puerto Rican theater group, Anamú and then director of the Puerto Rican Travelling Theater. He is at present also the producing director of Teatro Festival, a biennial gathering of Latino Theaters.

"The Caravan" / "La Caravana," based on the poem "La elegía del Saltimbanqui," is a charming script, which uses song and dance, and magic. It's theme is the abuse of power, which is described by role reversal. As the characters change costumes and roles, they change their attitudes. This leads to the understanding that a change of power does not always mean change of conditions, and frequently the assumption of power continues what was supposed to change. It is an adult theme, but expressed simply and delightfully, so that the play is really for all ages, including the very young.

Lisa Loomer

"Bocón!" is a bilingual script which uses such folkloric characters as La Llorona to present a modern theme of protest against dictatorial power of all kinds. Submissiveness, characterized by the loss of the ability to voice a protest, is the cardinal sin. The use of the chorus in a rhythmic, dance-like combination of single voices and a unified voice, drum beats and pantomimic movement can be fascinating. Another exciting element is song, characteristic of Miguel and of La Llorona. It is symbolic of the struggle between the individual and the bureaucracy, as is the symbolism in the struggle of night and day, light and darkness.

Manuel Martín, Jr.

Manuel Martín, Jr., who was born in Cuba, is very much a part of the New York scene. A graduate of Hunter College, he went on to study acting at the Strassberg Academy and the American Academy of Dramatic Arts, among others. He has written a number of plays, including musicals, which have had successful productions by INTAR, DUO and La Mama Experimental Theater. "The Legend of the Golden Coffee Bean," a play for children, had a long and successful run at the New York Children's Theatre. He has also written for film and television. At present he is playwright in residence at INTAR.

"The Legend of the Golden Coffee Bean," by Manuel Martín, Jr., with music by William Sakas, is a parable, leading to the conclusion that learning and sharing are treasures to be found only by those who cultivate their curiosity. The focus is on the child, Chomiha, who is in search of wealth. Gucumatz sends her on a mission to find the golden coffee bean, which will bring her that wealth. This search sends her from country to country in Latin America, with the result that she learns a good deal about the ways of each country, but returns to Gucumatz wondering if she will ever find the golden coffee bean. Gucumatz informs her that she has found it, for she is now infinitely richer than she was before.

It is a joyful script, indicating the magic of song, dance and pantomime as a way of dealing with the changes of time, space and the mounting frustrations that turn out to reverse themselves. And it is a wonderful way to teach geography to children.

Joe Rosenberg

Joe Rosenberg was born in Poland of Jewish parentage. He didn't learn to speak Spanish until he reached middle age, and until then knew very little about any aspect of Hispanic life. His marriage to Graciela de la Peña of Morelia, Michoacán, México, changed all that, because each member of the *pareja* wanted to assimilate the best of each other's culture and minimize the worst. One result was that Rosenberg, who was director of theater at

Goddard College in Plainfield, Vermont, after picking up a smattering of Spanish and considerable exposure to central Mexican culture, took an appointment with what is now Texas A & M University Kingsville to form the first university bilingual theater company in 1972. There, he and Graciela translated the award-winning play script, "Historias para ser Contadas," by Oswaldo Dragún. Eventually Graciela went full-time as professor at the University of Texas-Brownsville.

La Compañía de Teatro Bilingüe was formed at Kingsville in 1972; by 1973 it was touring Mexico and all over the United States with actors who performed in Spanish and English back-to-back. The Mexican tours were for six weeks every year, and usually resulted in some fifty performances in the university and professional circuits. By 1980, the group formed the professional Bilingual Theater Company of Corpus Christi, Texas.

"El Gato sin Amigos" / "The Cat who had No Friends" is unique for this anthology because it can at best lay claim to a fusion of heritages. The story comes from a Cuban picture book which was written to teach children the values of the Castro regime from the Castro viewpoint. Rosenberg received permission from the writer, Teresita Gómez Vallejo, to adapt this story for the theater. It underwent a transformation during rehearsals, partly because it was to be presented to an American public, partly because the story was better than its propaganda purpose, and mostly because the actors were South Texans—Mexican Americans and non-Hispanics—who had an experiential range very far from Cuban. They brought to the written characters, and also to those they invented, a viewpoint which is South Texan and, our experience tells us, universally American. So what shall this script be called? Cuban? Mexican American? Or Hispanic Intercultural?

Intercultural was our purpose. Just as Rosenberg and De la Peña undertook to understand each other's cultural background better, so we hoped, would those who experienced performances of "El Gato Sin Amigos" / "The Cat Who Had No Friends." Our ambition was that anybody, regardless of linguistic limitations, would be afforded the opportunity to enjoy this play. The script is designed to reach multicultural audiences, and as such has had more than 500 presentations all over Texas and in various other places.

"El Gato Sin Amigos" / "The Cat Who Had no Friends" is a bilingual play script written for any kind of staging, with a strong reliance upon audience interaction with the performers. At one point or possibly several points, the audience is invited on stage to perform. The style of writing is in a minor way reminiscent of the Renaissance Italian commedia dell' arte, in which the writer presented experienced actors with a brief, often one-page, description of the play and left the rest to the actors to invent what they would, in whatever of the many languages at their disposal that they chose to use. Each actor had a specialization of his own which permitted infinite improvisation, as well as stock routines called *lazzi*. In this script the director can use as many woodland characters as he/she wishes, and can permit each of the actors to invent through improvisation; but at the same time the basic story is developed and set. Another feature is that most of the actors do not speak but rather use pantomimic behavior. This makes it possible for actors who are monolingual, deaf, or other, to perform. After all, all cultural sets matter. The music, composed by John Matthew Rosenberg, is all for the purposes of background, but it captures the spirit of the action so well that it considerably increases the opportunity for pantomimic acting.

Héctor Santiago

Héctor Santiago was born in La Habana, Cuba. He is a graduate of the Seminario de Dramaturgia Nacional de Cuba. In 1959 he founded the children's theatrical movement. He worked in Havana as an actor, director, choreographer, dancer and did twenty plays as a puppeteer. He has been living in New York since 1978. Among his published works are *Las Noches de la Chamblona*, and *Madame Camille, Escuela de Danza*. He has received many awards for his work, and has had stories and poetry anthologized.

Héctor Santiago presented this work, with great success, in Cuba twenty years ago.

"El Día que Robaron los Colores" / "The Day They Stole All the Colors" is a script that is formed around the marionette style of theater. One great advantage of this kind of theater is that it offers freedom from the spatial limitations of the stage of human actors. Characters can move across the stage, disappear up into the heavens, descend from the heavens at will, and the audience takes it all in because of the magic involved in make-believe. But Héctor Santiago does not stop there. In this hilarious action that takes place throughout the entire universe, he delights the spectators with all kinds of surprises: live actors who behave as puppets, shadow pantomime, grotesqueries of all kinds, multi-media, the whole 9,000 yards. And it all adds up to a splendid spoof, Punch-and-Judy style, about stock heroes, American types, such as peg-legged pirates, lasso-twirling crooks of the cowboy variety and people who conform at the slightest suggestion.